Strange Alloy

*The Relation of Comedy to Tragedy
in the Fiction of Henry James*

The University of
North Carolina Press
Chapel Hill

Strange Alloy

*The Relation of Comedy to Tragedy
in the Fiction of Henry James*

by Ellen Douglass Leyburn

Foreword by
William T. Stafford

Publication of this book was assisted by
a grant from Agnes Scott College.

~ No themes are so human as those that reflect for us, out of the confusion of life, the close connexion of bliss and bale, of the things that help with the things that hurt, so dangling before us for ever that bright hard medal, of so strange an alloy, one face of which is somebody's right and ease and the other somebody's pain and wrong. To live with all intensity and perplexity and felicity in its terribly mixed little world would thus be the part of my interesting small mortal; bringing people together who would be at least more correctly separate; keeping people separate who would be at least more correctly together; flourishing, to a degree, at the cost of many conventions and proprieties, even decencies, really keeping the torch of virtue alive in an air tending infinitely to smother it; really in short making confusion worse confounded by drawing some stray fragrance of an ideal across the scent of selfishness, by sowing on barren strands, through the mere fact of presence, the seed of the moral life. [Preface to "What Maisie Knew," *The Art of the Novel: Critical Prefaces by Henry James,* ed. Richard P. Blackmur (New York, 1934), p. 143.]

Foreword

Ellen Douglass Leyburn's *Strange Alloy: The Relation of Comedy to Tragedy in the Fiction of Henry James* could be called an "unfinished" work only in a very limited, very special sense. It could be called unfinished by virtue of the sad fact that Professor Leyburn was unable to see the book through the press because of her death on March 20, 1966, shortly after she submitted the manuscript to The University of North Carolina Press and before she could be informed of its acceptance. It could also, I suppose, be called unfinished in the sense that had she lived she might have been persuaded to bring into her fine critical ken a more inclusive coverage of the comic and tragic at work in the fiction of Henry James. That is to say, she might have been persuaded to extend her acute knowledge of the novelist's fiction into additional Jamesian eddies and backwaters. All of which is to say, in one sense, only that to have done so well what she has done inevitably whets the appetite for more. And of which is *not* to say, in another sense, that what *is* done in this book is in

any major way incomplete, unfinished, or inconclusive. *Strange Alloy*, in all conventional senses, is a *completed* critical study. In it Professor Leyburn examined representative works from "A Tragedy of Error" (James's first short story) through *The Golden Bowl* (his last great novel). And her clearly articulated demonstration throughout, of the pervasive mixture, in James's fiction, of the "comic with the painful in human experience," makes of the study a signal contribution to the critical literature of this important American novelist.

Professor Leyburn was born in Durham, North Carolina, in 1907. She received her undergraduate degree from Agnes Scott College in 1927, her M.A. from Radcliffe the next year, and her Ph.D. from Yale University in 1934. In that same year she returned to Agnes Scott as a member of the English Department, in which she was advanced to professor in 1957, and of which she was appointed chairman in 1965. A gifted teacher and a respected scholar, she made many contributions to the critical history of Eighteenth Century English Literature, her field of special interest, most importantly, perhaps, in her *Satiric Allegory: Mirror of Man*, published by Yale University Press in 1956. Her training in, her thorough knowledge of, the Age of Reason—its sanity and clarity, its lucidity and discipline—appears to have been curiously fortuitous preparation for her approach to the fiction of Henry James.

I thus think *common-sensical* is perhaps the seminal word to use in first describing the achievement of Professor Leyburn's reading of Henry James, lead away a little, though it might, from the *imaginative* quality of her critique. A common-sense approach to Henry James, in spite of the reams of critical attention paid to his fiction, is a relatively rare occurrence. Professor Leyburn was never blind, for example, to the disparities between classical definitions of tragedy and comedy and the much looser senses in which James—as well as Professor Leyburn herself—uses the terms. We know exactly where we are through

the use of such quotes as James's own observation about "the way human levity hovers about the edge of all painful occurrences," or, indeed, the marvelous passages from the Preface to *What Maisie Knew* which serves both as epigraph to her critique and the source of its title: "No themes are so human as those that reflect for us, out of the confusion of life, the close connexion of bliss and bale, of the things that help with the things that hurt, so dangling before us forever that bright hard medal, of so strange an alloy, one face of which is somebody's right and ease and the other somebody's pain and wrong." And we know exactly where we are going when Professor Leyburn tells us that James's "rendering of this interaction" is her precise concern.

I think it also a common-sense virtue of her subject that James's concern with the mixture of the comic and the tragic is so demonstrably pervasive in his fiction. Even the casual reader of James is likely to remember his comments in the Preface to his first acknowledged novel—that to *Roderick Hudson*—that it was Rowland Mallet's "pathetic, tragic, comic, ironic, personal state" that held for James the greatest challenge. That same reader is likely to remember—at least when Professor Leyburn reminds him— that late in *The Portrait of a Lady* Isabel Archer is able to see that there is both comedy *and* tragedy in her realization of what her marriage to Gilbert Osmond truly is. And it is a sigh, "all comically, all tragically," that Maria Gostrey utters on the last page of *The Ambassadors*. In short, there is no question of the relevance of this subject to the early, middle, and late fiction of Henry James.

The knowledgeable Jamesian, finally, is not going to be surprised at what he discovers in this book. Its general movement, with perhaps one or two startling exceptions, is down generally predictable paths to more or less generally predictable conclusions. Yet, even for the expert, there are gratifying satisfactions all along the way: in the imagination of its organizational scheme, in its

meticulous scholarship, in its graceful style, and in its pertinent recognitions.

Her Introduction is what one would expect it to be: clear, lucid, specific. Chapter I, "Apprenticeship," is a brief survey of the earliest stories and that earliest novel, *Watch and Ward.* Chapter II, "Achievement of Artistic Mastery," examines precisely the major works one would anticipate: that is, *Roderick Hudson, The American,* "Daisy Miller," *Washington Square,* and, most importantly, *The Portrait of a Lady.* Perhaps one would not have anticipated, however, the beautifully convincing case (in the analysis of the last-named novel) of how the fate of Madame Merle embodies to perfection the tragic and the comic, or how Gilbert Osmond has himself been duped by Isabel no less than she by him. The next three chapters range much more freely, with illuminating conjunctions and juxtapositions of the most unexpected kind: from that of "The Pension Beaurepas," *The Reverberator,* and *The Golden Bowl,* for instance, as examples of "International Tragedy and Comedy" (Chapter III), to that of characters in *The Princess Casamassima, The Wings of the Dove,* and *The Ambassadors* as examples of "Partly Tragic Minor Characters" (Chapter V). A still different kind of conjunction is made in Chapter VI, that of Nanda Brookenham (of *The Awkward Age*) and Lambert Strether (of *The Ambassadors*), as examples of "The Troubled Life Mostly at the Centre of Our Subject," on the one hand, with that of Hyacinth Robinson (of *The Princess Casamassima*) on the other. And the freewheeling scope here is in fact even broader and more varied than these few instances suggest.

Chapter VIII is another matter, with a change in emphasis from character to technique, but with a reinforcement of theme through a most meticulous kind of special analysis of James's three late great novels. "The Use of the Word 'Funny' in the Late Novels" should startle and delight the Jamesian specialist no less than the casual reader. It will meaningfully inform both. And it would

have served well enough as a fitting cap to *Strange Alloy*. We have in addition, however, a beautifully revealing final chapter in which Professor Leyburn not only neatly recapitulated the "argument" of the whole; she also gained there an unexpectedly substantive kind of biographical perspective by way of an analysis of some of James's letters. Therein we also see clearly enough how his pervasive "awareness of tragedy is relieved by the rich play of wit and comic invention."

It is, indeed, the uniformly high quality of what we do have that provokes a little (for me) one nagging dissatisfaction. The fiction examined here is, to be sure, representative enough—early, middle, and late in James's career. Yet, there are great gaps in the canon that are touched only briefly or not at all. *What Maisie Knew* and "The Pupil," for example, are relegated to a footnote when, were they perhaps joined with the controversial "The Turn of the Screw," they could have constituted a beautiful case—and all with terms she had already set up—of the tragic comedy in James's stories of children. I am also a little disappointed that she did not see fit to apply her method to that most puzzling of all of James's novels, *The Sacred Fount*, for which she may well have had an especially appropriate key. There is no reference in the book to other late tragic comedies such as "The Beast in the Jungle," none, or very little, to the other rich examples among the stories of writers and artists, none to the many ghostly tales. In fact, the fiction she does examine, representative in one sense though it is, is pretty much restricted to relatively well-known examples—a decision that may well have been intentionally contrived and even, from one point of view, advantageous, although I think I see that decision as a limitation.

If, however, the specialist wants more, he can hardly help being pleased with the knowledgeable and scholarly care with which he has been presented with what he has in this book. Professor Leyburn knew her Henry James

very well indeed. And she also knew well the relevant scholarship on her subject.[1] She was obviously thoroughly familiar with Richard Poirier's study, the one book-length critique most immediately relevant to hers. She made appropriate acknowledgment to Sister M. Corona Sharp and Laurence Holland, authors of the two best most recent books on James that would disagree with part of what she has done. And she knew her James well enough not to be caught out on a limb with the special problem of James's revisions. (See her notes to her last two chapters.) I am impressed, moreover, with the fine way she used James's criticism, his Prefaces, and his famous essay on the art of fiction to give the appropriate kind of support to her conviction that James knew exactly what he was doing in this interacting area of comedy and tragedy. Her use of James's letters in her concluding chapter is precisely the critical coup her demonstration deserved and thus caps with a beautiful fitness the whole.

WILLIAM T. STAFFORD

Purdue University
W. Lafayette, Indiana
April, 1967

---

1. With possibly one curious exception: for Mary Kyle Michael's "Henry James's Use of the Word *Wonderful* in *The Ambassadors,*" *Modern Language Notes,* LXXV (February, 1960), 114-17, although only a note, would appear to have an immediate pertinency to Professor Leyburn's examination of the word *funny* in the late novels.

Preface

In the passage which I have chosen as epigraph, Henry James conveys not just the atmosphere of *What Maisie Knew*, about which he is writing, but his fundamental sense of life. The figure of alloy suggests not merely the presence and alternation of good and bad, but fusion and intermingling; correspondingly, in the figure of the medal with two faces, the same medal is simply seen on two different sides. Thus James's fiction portrays man and his state as a mingling of good and bad, with virtues sometimes turning into vices and great wrong sometimes producing right. Furthermore, he regards this human mixture sometimes comically, sometimes tragically, and sometimes with an irony so complex as to seem comic and tragic at once, as if he were showing both sides of the medal at the same time.

I am fully aware of the dangers in using the battle-scarred terms "tragedy" and "comedy" in discussing the work of Henry James. The critical argument over their definition is apparently endless; and James himself is

notoriously loose in his usage, especially of the word tragedy. It is unfortunate to have to use so highly charged a word for James's feeling of *lacrimae rerum;* but two considerations make its use inevitable. One is simply that no other term is available. The other is that James himself constantly used it in speaking of his sense of the grimness and complexity of human life. He is likely to use it for any sort of human evil or untoward circumstance which causes suffering. He is most interested in the suffering of his "free spirits," but he can use the word tragic to describe the misery of even his most limited protagonists. Thus tragedy is for him largely a matter of material. His sense of comedy, on the other hand, includes angle of vision, the way the material is viewed either by the author or by his creatures, to whom he often gives the power of a wry or sardonic humor as a way of dealing with their plights. The element of comedy lurks in both the situation and the presentation of it and often intensifies distress. In *The Ambassadors,* for instance, it is exactly Strether's awareness of the absurdity of his position which most sharpens its poignance both for himself and for the reader. In addition to this kind of comic intensification of the suffering of his free spirits, James also includes in his fiction a great many satiric pictures of people without perception—or, as he calls them "fools."

James apparently never defined comedy or tragedy; but he uses the words frequently in describing the "strange alloy" of human life. The meaning of both terms for him can be measured only by the multifarious representations which make up the sum of life in his fiction. Clearly his use of the words is broadly inclusive. The letter to Howells in which he promises to make *The Europeans* "a very joyous little romance" provides one of the few occasions when he contrasts comedy and tragedy. He begins by answering Howells' objection to the close of *The American:* "I quite understand that as an editor you should go in for 'cheerful endings'; but I am sorry that as a private reader

you are not struck with the inevitability of the *American* dénouement." After explaining why Claire de Cintré could not have married Newman, he continues: "No, the interest of the subject was, for me (without my being at all a pessimist) its exemplification of one of those insuperable difficulties which present themselves in people's lives and from which the only issue is by forfeiture—by losing something. It was cruelly hard for poor N. to lose, certainly: but *que diable allait-il faire dans cette galère?* We are each the product of circumstances and there are tall stone walls which fatally divide us." After this clue to at least one meaning which tragedy holds for him, he confesses his own predilection toward tragedy and then his response to comedy: "I don't think that 'tragedies' have the presumption against them as much as you appear to; . . . I suspect it is the tragedies in life that arrest my attention more than the other things and say more to my imagination; but, on the other hand, if I fix my eyes on a sun-spot I think I am able to see the prismatic colors in it."[1]

James is not, to be sure, offering Howells a definition of tragedy; but it is worth noting that the only criterion he suggests (other than the absence of a "cheerful ending," which both men take for granted) is the confrontation of people with "insuperable difficulties." From the situations of characters so confronted, both heroes and lesser figures, grows the predominantly somber feeling of his fiction. I am far from sharing the view of such critics as Constance Rourke and Quentin Anderson[2] that James is incapable of tragedy in the classic sense of the term, which he seems to me to achieve in both *The Portrait of a Lady* and *The Wings of the Dove;* but his attention was arrested by the tragedies of small people as well as great,

[1]. *The Selected Letters of Henry James,* ed. Leon Edel (New York, 1955), pp. 68-70.
[2]. Constance Rourke, *American Humor: A Study of the National Character* (New York, 1931), pp. 255-61; Quentin Anderson, *The American Henry James* (New Brunswick, 1957), *passim,* e.g., pp. 10, 133, 238.

and he arouses the tragic emotions of pity and fear for characters whom the strict theorist would regard as pathetic rather than tragic.

In James's *Partial Portraits,* there is a passage on Daudet which throws light on the relation of comedy to tragedy in his own fiction:

> It gives a sociability to his manner, in spite of the fact that he describes all sorts of painful and odious things. This contradiction is a part of his originality. He has no pretension to being simple, he is perfectly conscious of being complex, and in nothing is he more modern than in this expressive and sympathetic smile—the smile of the artist, the sceptic, the man of the world—with which he shows us the miseries and cruelties of life. It is singular that we should like him for that—and doubtless many people do not, or think they do not. What they really dislike, I believe, is the things he relates, which are often lamentable.[3]

James's smile is not Daudet's; but it is clearly the smile of the artist who is perfectly conscious of being complex. And his complexity is the greater for not being just in the relation of the presentation to the life presented. What he presents is itself a complicated interrelation of the tragic and the comic; and the more he looks at "the way human levity hovers about the edge of all painful occurrences,"[4] the more interconnection he sees. His comment on Daudet might be paraphrased to say that in nothing is Henry James more modern than in finding comedy and tragedy inseparable.

His affinity with the modern consciousness of complexity is indicated by the great number of critical studies which continue to appear, and it must serve as apology for this addition to the number. Although in discussing

3. "Alphonse Daudet," *Partial Portraits* (London, 1888), pp. 219-20.
4. Henry James, in a review of *A Foregone Conclusion* by W. D. Howells in the *North American Review* (January, 1875), reprinted in *Literary Reviews and Essays by Henry James,* ed. Albert Mordell (New Haven, 1957), p. 208.

the amalgam of laughter and pain in James's portrayal of the complexities of reality, one must perforce resort to the long used—and often abused—terms "comedy" and "tragedy," it is no part of my intention to offer a new definition of them, nor to justify James's own loose usage. What constantly interested him was the mixture and interaction of what he regularly calls comic with the painful in human experience. It is his rendering of this interaction which I wish to explore. I hope to show how he uses it to sharpen the intensity of a given work and how in the late works the contrasting elements are fused so as to give a still greater feeling of reality. It is the object of my study to show evolving in the early works James's power of relating comedy and tragedy and then to analyze examples of some of the ways in which as a mature artist he characteristically revealed the interconnections. Thus the arrangement of the first two chapters is chronological, whereas each of the remaining chapters discusses a particular element in James's portrayal of the tragic comedy of life, with examples chosen from the whole range of his fiction. In a body of writing so huge, the selection of examples is necessarily rigorous, and it may appear arbitrary. But I have tried to select works which are representative and will at once suggest parallels to those familiar with James's fiction. I hope that such readers will find something fresh in my analysis; but I have intended to give enough impression of the works under discussion to make the comments intelligible to those whose interest in James is just beginning. The happiest reward of my efforts would be to send readers to— or back to—James himself.

My own debt to earlier critics is quite literally immeasurable. I am conscious of special enlightenment both general and particular from some of the many fine studies of James's fiction; and I am sure that my response to him has been influenced in ways of which I am unconscious, during many years of reading in so rich a field. Sometimes the stimulus has been that of disagreement; but I have

tried not to break the movement of my own analysis by registering disagreements here. I have sometimes fancied the entry James might have made in his Notebooks of the "tragic, comic, *ironic* little subject" of the critical combats waged in his name. When I am conscious of specific indebtedness, I have, of course, acknowledged it in a footnote or in the text.

Other "airborne particles" of ideas which have come from years of discussing James's works both in and out of class with students and other friends are still harder to isolate and register, but equally valuable. It is, in fact, the questions and penetrating observations of students which are responsible for my launching on the present study. Among those who have helped me during the course of it, I wish to thank Miss Page Ackerman and Associate Professor Mary Rion for reading the manuscript; my sister, Mrs. A. E. Foster, who put it into legible shape and sustained me by her constant encouragement throughout its creation; Miss Anne Stapleton, who made the final typescript with endless skill and patience in reproducing James's idiosyncrasies of form; Miss Florence Smith, whose generosity in attending to multitudinous later details has made its publication possible; and Professor Clifford Lyons, whose friendly counsel advanced the book toward publication. I am grateful to President Wallace Alston and the Trustees of Agnes Scott College for a year's leave in which to write and to the American Council of Learned Societies for the Research Fellowship which made possible my spending some rewarding months reading the James Papers in the Houghton Library at Harvard University. To all the staff of the Reading Room there and to the librarians of the Agnes Scott College Library, I am indebted for unfailing and helpful kindness. I especially appreciate permission from Mr. John James of Cambridge to quote from two unpublished letters of Henry James.

ELLEN DOUGLASS LEYBURN
Agnes Scott College

Contents

Strange Alloy

The Relation of Comedy to Tragedy
in the Fiction of Henry James

I ~ Apprenticeship

The title of James's first tale "A Tragedy of Error"
is misleading in its Shakespearean echo, for the story contains no reverberations of the high spirits of Shakespeare's
youthful play. Neither does it show any promise of the
doubleness of attitude and subtlety of perception which
James himself was soon to develop. The luridness of the
melodrama in his presentation of the faithless wife contriving with a brutalized boatman to murder her trusting
husband is unrelieved. And the irony of the "error" by
which the lover instead of the husband is murdered is
obviously, and even arduously, contrived, with the pathetic
limp of the lame husband neatly used to provide by the
cane it necessitates the very sign on which the boatman
picks the wrong victim. Among the stories included in
the first volume of Edel's edition of *The Complete Tales
of Henry James,* covering the years from 1864 to 1868,
there are others as unrelievedly melodramatic as "A Tragedy of Error." Indeed, the last story in the volume, "De
Grey: a Romance," has the added grisly trappings of a
fatal curse upon the brides of the house of De Grey who

must die upon providing an heir and of absorption of the
life of the hero by his intended bride in a first crude
version of the theme to which James would revert in "Long-
staff's Marriage" and *The Sacred Fount.*

But in spite of the prevailing somberness of the
gloom of this apprentice work, there are traces in it of
James's feeling for comedy. "The Story of a Year," which
gives much more impression of reality than its predecessor,
is a curious mixture in handling, wavering between solemnity and mock solemnity. James gives, for instance, an
apparently perfectly straightforward account of Lizzie's
ghastly dream of the unburied corpse and her subsequent
brooding. Almost immediately, however, he assumes a
somewhat arch tone toward her; "No: the curtain had not
yet fallen, yet our young lady had begun to yawn. To
yawn? Aye, and to long for the afterpiece. Since the tragedy
dragged, might she not divert herself with that well-bred
man beside her?"[1] What follows, in its laughter at poor
Lizzie's brooding, reads almost like self-parody on James's
part: "Then she would cut her arm to escape from dismay
at what she had already done; and her courage would ebb
away with her blood, and, having so far pledged herself
to despair, her life would ebb away with her courage: and
then, alone, in darkness, with none to help her, she would
vainly scream, and thrust the knife into her temple, and
swoon to death. And Jack would come back, and burst
into the house, and wander through the empty rooms,
calling her name, and for all answer get a deathscent!
These imaginings were the more creditable or discredit-
able to Lizzie, that she had never read 'Romeo and Juliet' "
(I, 80-81). Clearly there are flickers here of James's sense
of comedy in the midst of tragedy. But there is no sign in
these earliest stories of his knowing how to make his comic

1. *The Complete Tales of Henry James,* ed. Leon Edel (New
York, 1961–   ), I, 79. This edition is the source of all references to
James's fiction in Chapter I. Hereinafter volume and page will be
given in parentheses after quotations.

awareness serve his artistic purpose. In "A Most Extraordinary Case," one of the most convincing of the early stories, James lets the invalid Mason give a self-mocking retort to his successful rival and then comments: "It is often said that, next to great joy, no state of mind is so frolicsome as great distress. It was in virtue of this truth, I suppose, that Ferdinand was able to be facetious" (I, 360). He thus very early makes explicit his awareness of the presence of mirth in sadness and the specific use of laughter as defense.[2] But in the early tales James's occasional sallies of wit, whether in dialogue or in author's comment, are rather awkwardly handled and are likely to seem as much an intrusion as does his generalized explanation of Mason's facetiousness.

The violence of the sensationalism in some of James's youthful work is so extreme as to seem ludicrous and thus introduces for the reader an element of unintended comedy. This is strikingly true of *Watch and Ward*, the first attempt at novel-length fiction, which reads almost like a collection of trite episodes from dime novel thrillers. Ripples of mirth, instead of shivers of horror, may be produced by the overwritten account of the frenzy and suicide of the heroine's father, the pathetic picture of her standing in her night dress orphaned and desolate, or her later frantic wanderings in the sinister streets of New York. James does not manage to invest any of the characters with the reality that he had already achieved in some of even the most awkwardly handled short fiction, so that the flat figures seem as ridiculous as the happenings. This first unsuccessful novel is probably James's most unredeemed descent into bathos; but bathos is still present in some of the tales in the second volume, 1868-72, of Edel's edition. "Master Eustace" and "Guest's Confession" are exaggerated enough in melodrama to miss their melo-

2. Richard Poirier calls attention to James's later and more successful use of the jest at moments of pain. (*The Comic Sense of Henry James*, p. 99.)

dramatic effect, though the second of them is too revolting
to raise any smile at its exaggeration. The most successful
tales in the volume are the wholly serious ones: "Gabrielle
de Bergerac" and "At Isella," in which James demonstrates
his power to deal convincingly with tenderness and passion
and to write with more mature control than he had been
capable of in "Poor Richard" and "A Most Extraordinary
Case," the movingly somber tales of the Civil War.

From the point of view of his development toward
a more complex attitude, however, the most interesting
tales of this period are "Osborne's Revenge," 1868, and "A
Light Man," 1869. In "Osborne's Revenge" the basis of
the story, Robert Graham's suicide under the delusion of
having been jilted by the innocent Henrietta Congreve and
Philip Osborne's plan to avenge his friend by winning
Miss Congreve's affections and jilting her in turn, is melodramatic enough. But the whole course of the revenge
from Osborne's falling in love at the first sight of the
lady,[3] through the successive encounters in which she
baffles and subdues him by her unconsciousness of wrongdoing, until he leaves her in the arms of the man to whom
she has been engaged all along: all of this is in the vein
of high comedy. James wins sympathy for Osborne in his
earnest obtuseness and at the same time shows his folly.
Furthermore, the story includes broad satire both of the
frivolous and malicious Mrs. Dodd, who is shown as the
source of the lie about Henrietta, and of the insipid Mr.
Stone, the caricatured clergyman placed by the remark:
"I suppose she's quite safe . . . she's with a clergyman"
(II, 35). In the course of a conversation extolling Henrietta's charms and virtues, Mr. Stone says to Philip:

3. The scene of the child rescued from his perch on the ocean-
surrounded rock and restored to his aunt inevitably suggests the
scene on the beach in "My Friend Bingham," 1867, where the child
is restored lifeless to his mother's arms and the man who has acci-
dentally killed the little boy falls in love with the mother and later
marries her. The difference in the degree of melodrama in the two
scenes is indicative of the different temper of the whole of the two
stories only a year apart.

"She sings sacred music with the most beautiful fervor."

"Yes, so I'm told. And I'm told, moreover, that she's very learned—that she has a passion for books."

"I think it very likely. In fact, she's quite an accomplished theologian. We had this morning a very lively discussion."

"You differed, then?" said Philip.

"Oh," said Mr. Stone, with charming *naïveté*, "*I* didn't differ. It was she!"

His fatuousness reaches its climax in the speech in which he repudiates the suggestion that she is a coquette:

"Well then, my dear sir"—and the young man's candid visage flushed a little with the intensity of his feelings—"I give you my word for it, that I believe Miss Congreve to be not only the most accomplished, but the most noble-minded, the most truthful, the most truly christian young lady—in this whole assembly."

"I'm sure, I'm much obliged to you for the assurance," said Philip. "I shall value it and remember it" (II, 38-39).

In such scenes, this early story contains gleams of the kind of mocking laughter which was to persist in James's work until the end, and in the treatment of Osborne there is a measure of the affectionate laughter which is equally characteristic. But underneath there is always the consciousness of the pathos of poor Graham's suicide, of which until the end Henrietta is as ignorant as she is innocent. We leave her sobbing in her lover's arms when she learns what everyone else in the story has known all along; and we leave Osborne thinking her still in ignorance, though he has been informed of the truth of Robert's obsession by Major Dodd, the brother-in-law of Mrs. Dodd, all too obviously lugged in for the purpose of giving information. The Major says:

"Well, then, my dear sir, she thinks he died in his bed. May she never think otherwise!"

In the course of that night—he sat out on the deck till two o'clock, alone—Philip, revolving many things, fervently echoed this last wish of Major Dodd (II, 60). Then comes the restoration to the comic mode in the final paragraph about Philip's marriage to a wife who resembles the photograph he has bought from a shop window in his vain attempt to arouse Henrietta's jealousy. The events of the tale are, to be sure, preposterous; but it marks a real advance in James's showing tragedy and comedy as mingled.

The doubleness in "A Light Man" is even more interesting. As Edel points out, James's intention "was to tell an autobiographical tale, in the form of a diary, in which the diarist would provide one picture of himself while the reader would form another" (II, 7). In carrying out this intention, he largely succeeds in making Max's self-complacency the instrument of his own satire of the ruthless cynicism with which the light man sets about replacing his generous friend Theodore in the affections of his benefactor. We occasionally see James's hand too plainly in what Max writes, as when he says, "More would be forgiven me if I had loved a little more, if into all my folly and egotism I had put a little more *naïveté* and sincerity" (II, 62). But for the most part the diary sounds like the authentic record of the writer's own reactions as he supplants Theodore. It fits the derisive comedy of the conception that after he has made himself indispensable to the old man and thinks he can achieve having the will remade in his favor, he is thwarted by his own rapacity and brings on the fatal illness of the decrepit miser. The scene in which he does this shows another level of the satire, for James is allowing the diarist consciously to show up the old man's greed and childishness as well as unconsciously to reveal himself in his sneers at the old reprobate whom he has fascinated. Max explains how carefully he chooses his opportunity and works on Mr. Sloane's feeling by saying that he must leave.

He felt the blow; it brought him straight down on his marrow-bones. He went through the whole gamut of his arts and graces; he blustered, whimpered, entreated, flattered. He tried to drag in Theodore's name; but this I, of course, prevented. But, finally, why, *why*, WHY, after all my promises of fidelity, must I thus cruelly desert him? Then came my trump card: I have spent my last penny; while I stay, I'm a beggar. The remainder of this extraordinary scene I have no power to describe: how the *bonhomme* touched, inflamed, inspired, by the thought of my destitution, and at the same time annoyed, perplexed, bewildered at having to commit himself to doing anything for me, worked himself into a nervous frenzy which deprived him of a clear sense of the value of his words and his actions; how I, prompted by the irresistible spirit of my desire to leap astride of his weakness and ride it hard to the goal of my dreams, cunningly contrived to keep his spirit at the fever-point, so that strength and reason and resistance should burn themselves out (II, 89).

He finally brings Mr. Sloane to the point of saying, "This is my will. . . . If you will stay with me I will destroy it" (II, 90). But he also brings him to the point of death. It is Theodore who finally destroys the will which has been made in his favor; and just afterward the fine recognition scene between the two young men is ended by the servant's entering to announce "that poor Mr. Sloane is dead in his bed!" (II, 96). The story ends appropriately with the diarist's deciding to wait on the spot to court the next of kin who has thus become the heir, "a maiden lady, . . . simply a discarded niece of the defunct" (II, 96).

"A Light Man" comes off very well as satire of both Max and Mr. Sloane. It is somewhat less successful in conveying the distress of the idealistic Theodore, who is

supposed to suffer more over the disillusion about his friend than over the loss of the fortune. He is given the added pathos of dependent sisters, and he worries about not doing his duty by them. "He thinks he ought to be with them—to be getting a larger salary—to be teaching his nieces." What Max calls "the poor boy's shrinking New England conscience" (II, 80) seems to take the form of worrying himself sick over Max's treachery and thus leaving the field clear for the complete alienation of the old man. James obviously intends to make him likable when he has Max speak of "his old unconscious purity and simplicity—that slender straightness which makes him remind you of the spire of an English abbey" (II, 64). But he remains as insipid for the reader as for Max. We resent Max's ruthless ousting of the friend who has taken him in; but the victim never seems quite real enough to win positive sympathy. Thus the story is much more effective as comedy than as tragedy; but it is a notable early attempt to combine the two, and at the same time it brings off the comedy successfully on more than one level. Furthermore, however little Theodore wins sympathy by his preternatural goodness, his suffering is directly caused by the evil which is being satirized. In this respect "A Light Man" seems to be an experiment in the use of comedy to define the evil which causes tragedy, a use more fully developed in *Daisy Miller* and recurring in later novels as part of the complex interaction of comedy and tragedy.

II ~ Achievement of Artistic Mastery

As James moved from apprenticeship to mastery, the rapid growth of his power to render the mingled comic and tragic effect of life is commensurate with the speed of his total development. *Roderick Hudson,* which James regarded as his first novel, shows an interpenetration of tragedy and comedy more marked than that in any of his earlier work. The opening scene sets the tone of high comedy, which Cecilia brings back whenever she comes in to fulfill her function of confidante for Rowland or to give information with her little satiric thumbnail sketches. In her account, Roderick's "mother is a widow, of a Massachusetts country family, a little timid, tremulous woman, always troubled, always on pins and needles about her son,"[1] whose interest in art frightens her because she has "a holy horror of a profession which consists exclusively, as she supposes, in making figures of people divested of all

1. *Roderick Hudson* (the New York Edition of *The Novels and Tales of Henry James*), p. 27. Unless otherwise specified, all subsequent references to the fiction of Henry James will be to this edition. Pages will be given in parentheses after quotations.

clothing" (p. 29). Mary Garland is "a young woman staying with his mother, a sort of far-away cousin; a good, plain, honest girl, but not a person to represent sport for the artistic temperament" (p. 30).

James does not limit his satiric wit to Cecilia's remarks as chorus. He writes gaily of Barnaby Striker, Esq., whose sculptured head showing "a gentleman with a pointed nose, a long close-shaven upper lip and a tuft on the end of his chin . . . betrayed comically to one who could relish the secret that the features of the original had often been at the mercy of an exasperated eye" (pp. 36-37). The lawyer is mocked by Roderick as part of the expression of his own rebellion: "Mr. Striker, you must know, is not simply a good-natured attorney who lets me dog's-ear his law-books. He 's a particular friend and general adviser. He looks after my mother's property and kindly consents to regard me as part of it" (p. 44). And James makes the lawyer behave in a way to bear out Roderick's account. His speeches to Rowland show exactly why Roderick has felt impelled to smash the statue of him as a first expression of freedom: "We are inspired with none but Christian sentiments," said Mr. Striker; "Miss Garland perhaps most of all. Miss Garland," and Mr. Striker waved his hand again as if to perform an introduction which had been frivolously omitted, "is the daughter of a minister, the granddaughter of a minister, the sister of a minister" (p. 57). His view of art is suggested by his comment: "An antique, as I understand it . . . is an image of a pagan deity, with considerable dirt sticking to it, and no arms, no nose and no clothing. A precious model, certainly!" (pp. 58-59). He sums himself up with relish: "I 'm a plain practical old boy, content to follow an honourable profession in a free country. I did n't go to any part of Europe to learn my business; no one took me by the hand; I had to grease my wheels myself, and such as I am, I 'm a self-made man, every inch of me!" (pp. 62-63). James is writing here with delighted gusto and his rendering of Striker pre-

pares for the more extended treatment of Mr. Leavenworth's different brand of American boastfulness in the
scenes in Roderick's Roman studio, where we hear him
order his "high-class statuary" (p. 193) and "enunciate the
principles of spiritual art—a species of fluid wisdom which
appeared to rise in bucketfuls, as he turned the crank,
from the well-like depths of his moral consciousness" (p.
269). James makes the unctuous roll of his pompous
periods almost audible: "I can conscientiously express myself as gratified with the general conception. . . . The figure
has considerable majesty and the countenance wears a fine
open expression. The cerebral development, however,
strikes me as not sufficiently emphasised. Our subject being, as we called it—did n't we?— Intellectual Refinement,
there should be no mistaking the intellect, symbolised
(would n't it be?) by an unmistakably thoughtful brow.
The eye should instinctively seek the frontal indications.
Could n't you strengthen them a little?" (pp. 303-4).

Cecilia's wit and the comic figures of Striker and
Leavenworth lend humor and variety to the novel and
might be regarded simply as comic relief, adding reality
only as they suggest the range of human life. But other
elements of comedy are more closely linked with the
tragedy. Perhaps the most broadly satirized character in
the novel is Mrs. Light, who is directly responsible for
Christina's corruption and thus for the particular direction
of Roderick's ruin. James's picture of her is steadily satiric
from the time of her appearance in the Villa Ludovisi:
"One was a woman of middle age, with a rather grand air
and a great many furbelows. She looked very hard at our
friends as she passed, and glanced back over her shoulder
as if to quicken the step of a young girl who slowly followed her. She had such an expansive majesty of mien that
Rowland supposed that she must have some proprietary
right in the villa and was not just then in a permissive
mood" (pp. 93-94). Her airs and graces, as well as her
agitations, James continues to mock; but concurrently with

the exposure of her folly and her ambition, he gives the spectacle of what these traits have done to Christina. In the brilliantly managed scene at Frascati, where Christina goes off with Roderick, displaying all her charm and her willfulness and her proud resentment of being pushed at the Prince by her mother, Mrs. Light's complaint and boast to Rowland are ironic in a way which is comic in its revelation of her, but tragic in its implications for Christina and for all the men who suffer because her mother has made her what she is:

> "The deuce knows whom she really cares for —even to me who have so known and so watched her she 's a living riddle. She has ideas of her own, and theories and views and inspirations, each of which is the best in the world until another is better. She 's perfectly sure about each, but they are fortunately so many that she can't be sure of any one very long. They may last all together, none the less, long enough to dish the Prince's patience, and if that were to happen I don't know what I should do. I should be the most miserable of women. It would be too cruel, after all I have suffered to make her what she is, to see the labour of years blighted by mere wicked perversity. For I can assure you, sir," Mrs. Light declared, "that if my daughter *is* the gifted creature you see, I deserve some of the credit for the creation" (pp. 247-48).

In the accounts of Mrs. Light's progress supplied by the wise Madame Grandoni, who serves for the Roman group something of the purpose Cecilia has fulfilled for the Northampton characters, there is always a strain of the sardonic toward the mother and of pity toward the daughter. Thus the satire of Mrs. Light is constantly linked with an awareness of the grave damage she has done to Christina and the suffering both of the daughter and of her lovers.

The satire is used as a means of defining the evil which is the precipitating cause of the tragedy.

The underlying cause is, of course, in Roderick's own nature. The possibility of both tragedy and comedy are implicit in him from the first. "He belonged to the race of mortals, to be pitied or envied according as we view the matter, who are not held to a strict account for their aggressions. Looking at him as he lay stretched in the shade, Rowland vaguely likened him to some beautiful, supple, restless, bright-eyed animal, whose motions should have no deeper warrant than the tremulous delicacy of its structure and seem graceful to many persons even when they should be least convenient" (pp. 31-32). But at first the implications of danger are given with a light irony which merely suggests apprehension. "He was radiant with good-humour, and his charming gaiety the evident pledge of a brilliant future" (p. 69). In the whole early part of the novel the comic-ironic tone predominates in the treatment of his deficiencies:

> Roderick's manners on the precincts of the Pincian were quite the same as his manners on Cecilia's verandah; they were no manners, in strict parlance, at all. But it remained as true as before that it would have been impossible, on the whole, to violate ceremony with less of lasting offence. He interrupted, he contradicted, he spoke to people he had never seen and left his social creditors without the smallest conversational interest on their loans; he lounged and yawned, he talked loud when he should have talked low and low when he should have talked loud. Many people in consequence thought him insufferably conceited and declared that he ought to wait till he had something to show for his powers before assuming the airs of a spoiled celebrity. But to Rowland and to most friendly observers this judgment was quite beside the mark and the savour

of the young man's naturalness as fine as good wine
(pp. 100-101).

James sustains the sense of the ludicrous in Roderick's lack of responsibility for his actions even after his
debauched sojourn in Baden-Baden and his easy mockery
have intensified the gravity of Rowland's concern. "The
young sculptor reverted to his late adventures again in the
evening, and this time talked of them more objectively,
as the phrase is; with a detachment that flowered little
by little into free anecdote—quite as if they had been the
adventures of some other, some different, ass. He related
half a dozen droll things that had happened to him, and,
as if his responsibility had been disengaged by all this
ventilation, wondered, with laughter, that such absurdities
could have been" (p. 140). And he is still speaking with
carefree detachment when he says, "I believe there 's a
certain group of circumstances possible for every man, in
which his power to choose is destined to snap like a dry
twig . . . . I 'm damnably susceptible, by nature, to the
grace and the beauty and the mystery of women, to their
power to turn themselves 'on' as creatures of subtlety and
perversity. So there you have me" (pp. 141-42). We soon
"have" him in his studio "revolving about Miss Light"
while Mrs. Light chatters to Rowland: "Ah, he 's gone to
look at my beautiful daughter; he 's not the first that has
had his head turned," the irrepressible lady resumed, lower-
ing her voice to a confidential undertone; a favour which,
considering the shortness of their acquaintance, Rowland
was bound to appreciate. "The artists are all crazy about
her. When she goes into a studio she 's fatal to the pictures.
And when she goes into the ball-room what do the other
women say? Eh, Cavaliere mio?" (p. 155). The crudity
of Mrs. Light's bad taste in saying it does not obscure the
truth of what she says. Roderick's downfall has begun;
and from this point on his decline is treated more and more
melodramatically. In the Preface written for the New York

Edition, James points out that "the time-scheme of the
story is quite inadequate, and positively to that degree
that the fault but just fails to wreck it . . . . Roderick's dis-
integration, a gradual process, and of which the exhibi-
tional interest is exactly that it *is* gradual and occasional,
and thereby traceable and watchable, swallows two years
in a mouthful, proceeds quite *not* by years, but by weeks
and months, and thus renders the whole view the dis-
service of appearing to present him as a morbidly special
case" (*The Art of the Novel*, p. 12). His precipitate moral
decline is concluded by his rushing to his physical death
in the spectacular Alpine storm. What is sacrificed in the
telescoping of presentation is the doubleness, and hence
the reality, which has marked the earlier impression. Once
Roderick begins to disintegrate, the comic balance is lost
in the rush; and the effect is exactly what James calls it:
"morbid."

But with Rowland, whose consciousness James declares is the "centre of interest throughout," the mixed
effect persists to the end. His goodness is the source of
his suffering; but his goodness is mingled with self-interest
and folly. He is pathetic when he says to Cecilia, "I want
to care for something or for somebody. And I want to
care, don't you see? with a certain intensity; even, if you
can believe it, with a certain passion . . . . Do you know I
sometimes think that I 'm a man of genius half-finished?
The genius has been left out, the faculty of expression is
wanting; but the need for expression remains, and I spend
my days groping for the latch of a closed door" (pp. 7-8).
But in trying to fulfill the needs of his nature through
Roderick, he makes a fool of himself and is then made a
fool of by others in a way that is both pitiful and comical.
His being foredoomed to failure is lightly suggested by
Cecilia's telling him candidly: "for a man who 's generally
averse to meddling, you were suddenly rather officious"
(p. 47), and warning him "that you 're likely to have your
hands rather full" (p. 48). Rowland himself is devoid of a

sense of humor, sober as he is by temperament and brought up by a father who "had been a man of an icy smile and a stony frown" (p. 9) to "habits marked by an exaggerated simplicity which was kept up really at great expense" (p. 12) and by a mother who "had been for fifteen long years a woman heavily depressed" (pp. 13-14). Consequently, his own apprehension is wholly serious: "when he reflected that he was really meddling with the simple stillness of this small New England home and that he had ventured to disturb so much living security in the interest of a far-away fantastic hypothesis, he gasped, amazed at his temerity. It was true, as Cecilia had said, that for an unofficious man it was a singular position. There stirred in his mind an odd feeling of annoyance with Roderick for having so peremptorily taken possession of his nature" (p. 67). He is, of course, trying to take possession of Roderick's, though he consciously wants only to free the young artist to develop. Roderick makes clear his own sense of the relation when he rather brutally declines Rowland's company on the vacation Rowland has suggested to restore the young man's artistic energies after the magnificent creation of his first winter's work in Rome:

> "I think my journey will do me more good if I take it alone. I need n't say I prefer your society to that of any man living. For the last six months it has been a fund of comfort. But I 've a feeling that you 're always expecting something of me, that you 're measuring my doings by a terrifically high standard. You 're watching me, my dear fellow, as my mother at home watches the tea-kettle she has set to boil, and the case is that somehow I don't want to be watched. I want to go my own way; to work when I choose and to be a fool, to be even a wretch, when I choose, and the biggest kind of either if necessary. It 's not that I don't know what I owe you; it 's not that we are not the best friends in the world. It 's simply—it 's simply—!"
>
> "It 's simply that I bore you," said Rowland (p. 127).

Throughout the novel James keeps Rowland the same suffering, long enduring friend, who *is* something of a bore, and who cannot supply the deficiency in his nature by any satisfactory relation with others. As the Preface points out, his falling in love with Mary Garland is not adequately developed; but his behavior toward her is exactly consistent with his forebearance toward Roderick. However noble his self-effacement and his efforts to keep Roderick up to the mark as a lover, even after the youth's artistic power has failed, there is something comic as well as pathetic in his position vis-à-vis Mary, and his patience, which is the last impression in the novel. The cry with which Mary had flung herself on the lifeless body of Roderick

> still lives in Rowland's ears. It interposes persistently against the consciousness that when he sometimes—very rarely—sees her, she is inscrutably civil to him; against the reflection that during the awful journey back to America, made of course with his assistance, she had used him, with the last rigour of consistency, as a character definitely appointed to her use. She lives with Mrs. Hudson under the New England elms, where he also visits his cousin Cecilia more frequently than of old. When he calls on Mary he never sees the elder lady. Cecilia, who, having her shrewd impression that he comes for the young person, the still young person, of interest at the other house as much as for anyone else, fails to show as unduly flattered, and in fact pronounces him, at each reappearance, the most restless of mortals. But he always says to her in answer: "No, I assure you I 'm the most patient!" (pp. 526-27).

The importance of the character of Rowland in the development of James's method of focusing on a center of consciousness within his fiction has often been pointed out. Rowland seems equally important in the development of his power to render the mingled tragedy and comedy of life and to show them enhancing each other. It is significant that in the paragraph of the Preface where he declares

that Rowland's consciousness is the center of interest, he
discusses exactly this mixture in him:

> It had, naturally, Rowland's consciousness, not to
> be *too* acute—which would have disconnected it and
> made it superhuman: the beautiful little problem
> was to keep it connected, connected intimately, with
> the general human exposure, and thereby bedimmed
> and befooled and bewildered, anxious, restless, falli-
> ble, and yet to endow it with such intelligence that
> the appearances reflected in it, and constituting to-
> gether there the situation and the "story," should
> become by that fact intelligible. Discernible from
> the first the joy of such a "job" as this making of
> his relation to everything involved a sufficiently lim-
> ited, a sufficiently pathetic, tragic, comic, ironic, per-
> sonal state to be thoroughly natural, and yet at the
> same time a sufficiently clear medium to represent
> a whole (*The Art of the Novel,* p. 16).

The James who wrote the prefaces for the New York Edition had already created more acute and yet poignantly
limited centers of consciousness; but even without the
Preface, we might be able to see in Rowland's "limited . . .
pathetic, tragic, comic, ironic personal state" the promise
of the fusion of tragedy and comedy in such a moving late
character as Lambert Strether.

～   ～   ～

Roderick Hudson vividly re-creates the European
scene in which James began work on it; and part of its
charm lies in its power to evoke the impression of Italian
light, of the cool dimness behind the heavy leather of
church entrances, of the very fragrance of the sun-warmed
pines. Furthermore, all that "Europe" means to an American, and especially to an artist, operates in the story as
far more than setting. But it is not until *The American*
that James uses the relation of the two cultures to create the

special connection between comedy and tragedy. The juxtaposition of Newman's American, naïve self-confidence with the narrow family pride of the de Bellegardes is exactly the source of both the comedy and the tragedy of the novel. The comedy of the superb scene in which Newman is introduced to the old marquise has been admirably analyzed by Richard Poirier;[2] but the same scene is full of tragic implications. Indeed, the sense of inevitable disaster for Newman in the relation he is seeking to establish gives peculiar intensity to the wit.

> "Do you like Paris?" asked the old lady, who was apparently wondering what was the proper way to talk to an American.
> "I think that must be the matter with me," he smiled. And then he added with a friendly intonation: "Don't *you* like it?"
> "I can't say I know it. I know my house—I know my friends—I don't know Paris."
> "You lose a great deal, as your daughter-in-law says," Newman replied.
> Madame de Bellegarde stared; it was presumably the first time she had been condoled with on her losses. "I'm content, I think, with what I have," she said with dignity. Her visitor's eyes were at this moment wandering round the room, which struck him as rather sad and shabby; . . . He ought obviously to have answered that the contentment of his hostess was quite natural—she had so much; but the idea did n't occur to him during the pause of some moments which followed (*The American,* pp. 185-86).

The placing together of the two kinds of self-complacency, with each speaker incomprehensible to the other, is humorous indeed; and the scene grows more broadly satirical as Newman meets the sneers in M. de Bellegarde's increasingly condescending questions without betraying any recognition of being patronized. When the old marquise, pretending to misunderstand his boast that his sister is

2. *The Comic Sense of Henry James,* pp. 70 ff.

married to the owner of the largest india-rubber house in the West inquires, "Ah, you make houses also of india-rubber?" Newman indulges in what James calls a "burst of hilarity" (p. 193).

The exchange is hilarious; but it also carries a shudder of tragic apprehension for Newman. We feel that Madame de Bellegarde's wit should put him on guard more even than the declaration which comes when he is left alone with her: "You don't know what you ask. I 'm a very proud and meddlesome old person" (p. 197). He makes the best possible answer: "Well, I 'm very rich," and she seems to capitulate. But it is the comic scene which has showed the measure of his antagonist, a measure which Newman himself has not fully taken. The comedy conveys the sinister, which is soon to become melodramatic; and yet Newman stays within the comic frame.

In the presentation of Newman's pride, James uses tolerant laughter to keep the American from being objectionable; but the laughter accentuates both the kind and the degree of his self-confidence. In the scene in which Valentin has tried to warn him of the difficulties of his suit for the hand of the daughter of the ancient house, he shows himself totally incapable of understanding that their being of the nobility and his having manufactured wash tubs would matter to the de Bellegardes. In the New York Edition James drops his declaration, "I simply think, if you want to know, that I 'm as good as the best";[3] but all his speeches show that this is what he thinks. James engages affection for Newman in part exactly by making him somewhat ridiculous in his inability to understand what Valentin is telling him: "Well, I give you warning again. . . . My mother's strange, my brother's strange, and I verily believe I 'm stranger than either. You 'll even find my sister a little strange. Old trees have crooked branches, old houses have queer cracks, old races have odd secrets.

3. *The American*, Rinehart Edition, ed. Joseph Warren Beach (New York, 1949), p. 110.

Remember that we 're eight hundred years old!" (p. 162). Newman is presented in the round; and his admirable and lovable qualities lift him quite out of the company of Striker and Leavenworth; but the blindly naïve American pride which he shares with them is at once his tragic flaw and his comic weakness.

The pride of the de Bellegardes is of a wholly different order and is the basis of James's severest satire and extremist melodrama. *The American* suffers somewhat as does *Roderick Hudson* by the too sudden shift from comedy to melodrama; and the whole sequence of the final action is too lurid to be credible. The repudiation of Newman by the de Bellegardes after the public proclamation of his engagement at their great ball, the retirement of Claire to the convent which Newman sees as a prison, Valentin's death after the duel over the contemptible Mlle. Nioche, his sending Newman to Mrs. Bread to learn the awful secret of the murder which will give him power over Madame de Bellegarde: the sensations follow pell-mell upon one another and rush to the conclusion of Newman's magnanimous refusal of his revenge. Such credibility as the last part of the novel retains is due to the way James has, to use his own phrase, "set Newman on his feet" by the mixed view of him and to the defining by satire of the evil which figures in the melodrama of the de Bellegardes. The cutting of the cable which ties "the balloon of experience" to earth, James points out with delightful candor in the Preface. "The way things happen is frankly not the way in which they are represented as having happened, in Paris, to my hero: . . . My subject imposed on me a group of closely-allied persons animated by immense pretensions —which was all very well, which might be full of the promise of interest: only of the interest felt most of all in the light of comedy and of irony" (*The Art of the Novel*, pp. 33, 34-36). James, at the distance from which he writes the prefaces, explains what would have preserved the artistic integrity as well as the sense of reality in the novel:

"This, better understood, would have dwelt in the idea
not in the least of their not finding Newman good enough
for their alliance and thence being ready to sacrifice him,
but in that of their taking with alacrity everything he
could give them, only asking for more and more, and then
adjusting their pretensions and their pride to it with all
the comfort in life" (*The Art of the Novel*, p. 36). The
delectable scenes of satire and of a complicated predicament for Newman suggested in this account of the possible
progress of the novel can only increase dismay over the
"affront to verisimilitude" (*The Art of the Novel*, p. 37)
in its actual progress, where the loss of tragic power is in
exact proportion to the absence of comedy.

~   ~   ~

In *Daisy Miller*, James sustains the feeling of verisimilitude by retaining to the end the mingling of comedy
and tragedy. The source of both is again the incomprehension created by limiting social perspectives; but James
handles with much greater assurance the conflict of manners out of which the complications spring. Without ever
overcrowding his small canvas, he includes an astonishing
range of comedy within the narrow frame he has chosen.
This he accomplishes partly by the economy with which he
serves two purposes at once in showing the impudence of
the irrepressible Randolph, the fatuous permissiveness of
Mrs. Miller, and even the homekeeping industry of the
father Ezra B. Miller who, as Randolph proclaims, is in a
"better place than Europe . . . . My father's in Schenectady.
He's got a big business. My father's rich, you bet!" (*Daisy
Miller*, p. 13). The Millers provide broad comedy in themselves, but at the same time they help to explain Daisy's
innocence, which is both comic and tragic. There is equal
artistic economy in the treatment of Daisy. The perfect
good humor with which she defies the conventions by her

late entrance at Mrs. Walker's party, where "she rustled forward in radiant loveliness, smiling and chattering, carrying a large bouquet and attended by Mr. Giovanelli" (p. 68), makes Mrs. Walker's consternation very funny; but it is also the portent of the bewilderment and pain with which Daisy receives the rebuff of Mrs. Walker's turning her back at the end of the party and finally ostracizing the little American girl from Roman-American society. Daisy is the more pathetic because she remains comically unaware of what she has done in violating the proprieties of which she acknowledges neither the power, nor indeed the existence.

It is another mark of James's economy in making the comedy enforce the tragedy that he uses exactly this innocent, ignorant, and yet authentically perceptive, Daisy to reveal the wrongness of the standard by which she is judged, both when she tells Mrs. Walker, who is trying to keep her from walking with Giovanelli, "I never heard anything so stiff! If this is improper, Mrs. Walker, . . . then I 'm *all* improper, and you had better give me right up" (pp. 62-63), and in the conversation at the party when she tells Winterbourne that he is "stiff":

> "You say that too often," he resentfully remarked.
> Daisy gave a delighted laugh. "If I could have the sweet hope of making you angry, I'd say it again."
> "Don't do that—when I'm angry I'm stiffer than ever. But if you won't flirt with me do cease at least to flirt with your friend at the piano. They don't," he declared as in full sympathy with "them," "understand that sort of thing here."
> "I thought they understood nothing else!" cried Daisy with startling world-knowledge.
> "Not in young unmarried women."
> "It seems to me much more proper in young unmarried than in old married ones," she retorted.
> "Well," said Winterbourne, "when you deal with natives you must go by the custom of the country" (p. 71).

It is a proof of James's artistry in conveying the contradictory truth of life that he makes both of these incom-
patible views seem sound.

The person whom he shows as totally wrong in her
judgment of Daisy is Mrs. Costello: "a person of much
distinction and who frequently intimated that, if she had n't
been so dreadfully liable to sick-headaches she would probably have left a deeper impress on her time" (p. 22). James
never lets her pronounce Daisy "common" without satirizing Mrs. Costello herself, as when he makes her say, "She
has that charming look they all have . . . . I can't think
where they pick it up; and she dresses in perfection—no,
you don't know how well she dresses. I can't think where
they get their taste" (pp. 23-24). But in his mockery of
Mrs. Costello's snobbishness, James is also establishing the
attitude which is to cause the suffering; and in the hurt she
administers by refusing to meet Daisy, he gives the first
hint of the tragedy with which the whole comedy of manners is instinct.

It is also Mrs. Costello who first confuses Winterbourne's judgment. His bewilderment is, throughout, the
focus of the novel; the fluctuations of his feeling make him
ridiculous, but they also prevent his really falling in love
with the adoring and adorable Daisy and thus saving her
from destruction. The gradations of his susceptibility and
his uneasiness waver from his initial question "Was she
simply a pretty girl from New York State? . . . Or was she
also a designing, an audacious, in short an expert young
person?" (p. 17) through his response to every subsequent
meeting. "It was the most charming innocent prattle he had
ever heard. . . . If he had assented to the idea that she was
'common,' at any rate, *was* she proving so, after all, or
was he simply getting used to her commonness?" (p. 40).
And so he wonders on, coming back always "to the dreadful
question of whether this *was* in fact a nice girl" (p. 58).
"It struck him also that Daisy had never showed to the eye
for so utterly charming; but this had been his conviction on

every occasion of their meeting" (p. 81). He continues to fluctuate until he finally decides, on seeing her with Giovanelli in the Colosseum by moonlight, that she is wholly bad and that he "need no longer trouble his head or his heart" about her (p. 86). The vacillations are so adroitly presented that they seem to last over a much longer period than the actual time span of the novel.[4] So reiterated, and yet so varied, is Winterbourne's worrying of the question that it seems much more extended than it is; and it is, as much as the naturalness of Daisy's own behavior, what saves the novel from the feeling of too great foreshortening which mars the last half of both *Roderick Hudson* and *The American*. Winterbourne's comical inability to trust his own feeling about Daisy is enforced by his recognition that he had "lived at Geneva so long . . . [that] he had lost the right sense for the young American tone . . . . his instinct . . . had ceased to serve him, and his reason could but mislead" (pp. 16-17). His bewilderment emphasizes the power of the forms which govern the expatriate society to which he belongs as well as his own ridiculous subservience to them. His awareness that this is a matter about which he needs to be able to trust his feeling and yet his continuing to worry it with his reason give the nouvelle the special quality of irony which makes it lifelike. It seems peculiarly fitting that it should require Giovanelli, whom Winterbourne has judged with assurance as "anything but a gentleman" (p. 58), to speak the words at Daisy's funeral which give Winterbourne the final revelation that the "lady" is innocent. The end for Winterbourne is as ambiguous and as true to life as his ruminations have been throughout convincing in their tragic comedy. He comes back to the judgment: " 'I was booked to make a mistake. I 've lived too long in foreign parts.' . . . Nevertheless, he soon went back to live at

---

4. They operate in somewhat the same way as do Hamlet's soliloquies to give the feeling of brooding over an extended period which makes the actual speed of the action seem credible.

Geneva, whence there continue to come the most contradictory accounts of his motives of sojourn: a report that
he's 'studying' hard—an intimation that he's much interested in a very clever foreign lady" (pp. 93-94).

~   ~   ~

In the years immediately following the publication
of *Daisy Miller*, James produced a wide variety of works
in which he extended the range of interplay between tragedy and comedy. In the brilliant high comedy of "An
International Episode" and *The Europeans* the implications
of tragic possibilities give edge to the laughter. Indeed,
according to James's letter of explanation to Lizzie Boott[5]
it was only Howells' insistence on a tale with a happy ending which made him round out *The Europeans* with the
neat pairing off of couples which suggests the final dance
of Elizabethan comedy. And even deference to Howells
did not make him obscure the wryness of the solitary departure of the countess, the most interesting character in
the novel and the one whom he had handled throughout
with the most intricate and fascinating mixture of tragedy
and comedy.

In *Washington Square* the balance is once more
toward tragedy intensified by comedy. Catherine Sloper's
bringing home "her undiverted heart"[6] to her faithless lover
is the more moving because James has demonstrated that

5. "I do incline to melancholy endings—but it had been a part
of the bargain with Howells that *this* termination should be cheerful and that there should be distinct matrimony. So I did it off
mechanically in the closing paragraphs. I was not at all weary of
the tale at the end, but I had agreed to write it in *100 Atlantic* pages,
& its abrupt ending came from outward pressure—not from internal
failing." James Papers in the Houghton Library, Harvard University
b MS Am 1094, No. 543. Henry James to Lizzie Boott, Oct. 30 [1878].

6. *Washington Square*, Modern Library Edition (New York, 1950),
p. 204. Since Henry James did not include *Washington Square* in
the New York Edition, all references to it are to the Modern Library
Edition.

"Mrs. Penniman had not made a clever woman of her" (p. 15). Mrs. Penniman, with her romantic dreams of a clandestine marriage for the "guilty couple," after which "they would be reconciled to her brother in an artistic tableau, in which she herself should be somehow the central figure" (p. 126), is one of the chief sources of humor in the novel; but her emptiness and incomprehension also increase the feeling of Catherine's loneliness in the fluttering presence of her aunt. In Dr. Sloper, who "almost never addressed his daughter save in the ironical form" (p. 33), James creates the chief means both of revealing Catherine's limitations and of intensifying her suffering. And all the while the clever ironist is himself the object of ironical satire. He can explain with perfect lucidity to Morris Townsend's sister: "A bad husband would have remarkable facilities for making her miserable; for she would have neither the intelligence nor the resolution to get the better of him, and yet she would have an exaggerated power of suffering," at the same time that he is driving her by his mockery into Morris's arms (p. 111). He discovers finally that she is "obstinate" (p. 273). But he never understands that he himself has broken her heart, that "she had heart enough for that" (p. 158). Toward Catherine James himself sustains a doubleness of tone in which the surface laughter shows the tenderness: "according to her aunt's expression, [she] went plumping down into the paternal presence. She was really too modest for consistent pathos. . . . Poor Catherine was conscious of her freshness; it gave her a feeling about the future which rather added to its weight upon her mind. It seemed a proof that she was strong and solid and dense, and would live to a great age—longer than might be generally convenient" (pp. 158, 159). It is this delicate balance of tone in the treatment of Catherine's suffering which keeps the sensationalism of her pursuit and betrayal by the fortune hunting Townsend from destroying the credibility of the novel. In the handling of the adventurer there is no

sudden shift from satire to melodrama such as has marred the presentation of the de Bellegardes. Morris is a preposterous figure of cardboard from his first flattering of Mrs. Penniman to his last petulant, "That was a precious plan of yours!" (p. 290) when he has found the middle-aged Catherine impervious to his worn-out histrionics. And the fact that he has accepted the foolish Mrs. Penniman as an accomplice has helped to make a fool of him all along. But it is the steady tone of mingled pathos and irony in James's treatment of Catherine which makes credible and moving both her having been hoodwinked by the claptrap of Morris' pretenses and the dignity and fortitude with which she "became an admirable old maid" (p. 267). It persists through the very last sentence in which James consigns her to needlework after her final dismissal of Morris: "Catherine, meanwhile, in the parlor, picking up her morsel of fancy-work, had seated herself with it again— for life, as it were" (p. 291).

～   ～   ～

In the whole range of his fiction during his early London years, even in the rather perfunctory *Confidence* and the most romantic of the tales such as "The Last of the Valerii," James seems to be experimenting with various interactions of tragedy and comedy. In the light of the event, and indeed of references in the letters to a major work which is to come, all of these pieces—however masterly their own achievement—show James preparing himself for the profound rendering in *The Portrait of a Lady* of the comedy and tragedy of life as interdependent. The different ways in which he has already demonstrated the interplay are now combined in a single work, "one, entire, and of a certain magnitude."

The very magnitude is, of course, partly what makes possible the greater richness of the representation. The

novel is, as James says in the Preface, making an "ado" about Isabel. But the size of the ado enables him to show a multiplicity of facets in his picture which would have shattered the tight frame of *Daisy Miller*. In this "spacious house," there is room even for the gay comedy of Henrietta Stackpole, with her round button eyes, looking always for the "inner life" and asking impertinent questions of Ralph and Lord Warburton. The depiction of Henrietta has more than is common in James of "the air of comedy comparatively free from sharp under-tastes" (*The Art of the Novel*, p. 138); but it is her comically practical observation, "The great thing is that he should n't die in the cars" (*The Portrait of a Lady*, II, 303), which makes more painful the fact that Ralph is going home to die. At the end it is she who, with her absurdly unwarranted optimism, adds the last bitterness to Goodwood's defeat.

> "Look here, Mr. Goodwood," she said; "just you wait!"

> On which he looked up at her—but only to guess, from her face, with a revulsion, that she simply meant he was young. She stood shining at him with that cheap comfort, and it added, on the spot, thirty years to his life. She walked him away with her, however, as if she had given him now the key to patience (II, 437-38).

More significantly, all through the novel, her judgments of Isabel, however comical in delivery, are sound and ominous.

Mrs. Touchett and her "little moral account-book —with columns unerringly ruled and a sharp steel clasp— which she kept with exemplary neatness" (I, 291), extends the range of comedy in the opposite direction from that of Henrietta's energetic effort to save Isabel from her fate. The comedy with which James presents her dry asperity has consistently very "sharp under-tastes": "Mrs. Touchett . . . now arrived and addressed herself to the tea-pot. Her greeting to her niece did not differ materially from her manner of raising the lid of this receptacle in order to

glance at the contents: in neither act was it becoming to make a show of avidity" (I, 247). The detached old lady, who declares of Isabel, "I shall do absolutely nothing with her, and she herself will do everything she chooses" (I, 59), controls her destiny as the meddlesome Henrietta never does. "It suddenly struck her that if her Aunt Lydia had not come that day in just that way and found her alone, everything might have been different" (II, 404). But in the texture of the novel she is woven into the meaning of Isabel's experience in a much more intricate way than simply initiating the trip to Europe. Her whole life of self-protection, which James reveals through comedy, is itself sad; and Isabel pities her as she perceives "how it had come over her dimly that she had failed of something, that she saw herself in the future as an old woman without memories" (II, 407). James places her bleak refusal of life beside Isabel's mistaken commitment with a significance that is lost neither upon Isabel nor upon the reader. And similarly, through all the range of characters from the Misses Molyneux "encased in sealskin jackets" (I, 104) to the Countess Gemini, whose "attire . . . had the look of shimmering plumage" (I, 365), the comic treatment, with or without "sharp under-tastes," is relevant to Isabel's own complexity.

Just as the interplay of amiable and sharp in the presentation of minor characters has a wider range than in any earlier work, so the treatment of international differences has more depth. The doubleness of its implications is emphasized by James's making both the best character and the worst expatriate Americans and letting Madame Merle point out the parellel: "Mr. Ralph Touchett: an American who lives in Europe" and "Gilbert Osmond —he lives in Italy; that's all one can say about him or make of him" (I, 280, 281). Ralph's father had found it a "very soluble . . . problem to live in England assimilated yet unconverted" (I, 49); but he had come to Europe as a grown man with his character fixed by Rutland, Vermont,

whereas Ralph and Osmond have both been exposed from childhood to the "high civilisation" of Europe. Madame Merle herself, whose birth James places with a special exuberance of humor in the "Brooklyn navy-yard" (I, 249), has left America in babyhood and seems to account for her origin more accurately when she says, "I was born before the French Revolution. Ah, my dear, *je viens de loin;* I belong to the old, old world!" (I, 279).

This "rare, superior and preëminent" (I, 267) woman had to "Isabel's imagination a sort of greatness. To be so cultivated and civilised, so wise and so easy, and still make so light of it—that was really to be a great lady" (I, 272). James has used Ralph to create uneasiness about Madame Merle who, he tells Isabel, is "the cleverest woman I know, not excepting yourself" (I, 251). His mistrust prepares an ironic response to Mrs. Touchett's saying, "I've asked her to put in this time because I wish you to know her. I think it will be a good thing for you. Serena Merle has n't a fault" (I, 277). The real irony, of course, the comedy of the tragedy, is that in one way she *is* a "good thing" for Isabel, whom she helps to educate, as do Ralph and Osmond himself. And there is the very truth of comedy in the fact that Isabel would hardly have been susceptible to Osmond's aestheticism without Ralph's training of her aesthetic taste. She wishes when she finally sees Osmond's treasures that she had been more prepared!

The richness of the European scene itself is most responsible for the educating of Isabel's American sensibilities, enlightening her just enough to make her an easy victim to the machinations of Madame Merle and Osmond and then helping to complete her education through suffering. James uses her response to successive places to mark the stages of her development from her first entrance into the mellow atmosphere of the lawn at Gardencourt, where the leisured teatime seems to promise "an eternity of pleasure" (I, 1). "The quality of this small ripe country seemed as sweet to her as the taste of an October pear"

(I, 83). And it is partly her very response to such ripeness which makes her know that her own "system and . . . orbit" (I, 144) will not fit into Lord Warburton's. She is looking with her very American eyes when she looks into those of Miss Molyneux and seems to see "in their grey depths the reflexion of everything she had rejected in rejecting Lord Warburton—the peace, the kindness, the honour, the possessions, a deep security and a great exclusion" (I, 189).

When she starts out to see more of the world, she examines with the same eagerness to receive impressions, to understand, and to judge which she has shown in studying the pictures in the gallery at Gardencourt. In London, she "was full of premises, conclusions, emotions; if she had come in search of local colour she found it everywhere" (I, 198). In Paris, where Mrs. Touchett introduces her "to the little circle of her fellow countrymen—dwelling upon the skirts of the Champs Elysées," she asks so American a question that her aunt attributes it to Henrietta's influence: "You all live here this way, but what does it lead to?" (I, 302). San Remo she views as the "threshold of Italy, the gate of admirations. Italy, as yet imperfectly seen and felt, stretched before her as a land of promise, a land in which a love of the beautiful might be comforted by endless knowledge" (I, 320). In Florence, she listens to arguments between Ralph and Madame Merle over details of paintings "with a sense that she might derive much benefit from them and that they were among the advantages she could n't have enjoyed for instance in Albany" (I, 354). There is still laughter in James's presentation of her pursuit of European culture when he says, "She performed all those acts of mental prostration in which, on a first visit to Italy, youth and enthusiasm so freely indulge" (I, 354). But a sinister undertone has come into the comedy of Europe enlightening American ignorance. Osmond's house, whose front is a mask, with "heavy lids, but no eyes" (I, 325), has already been introduced; and Isabel's

mornings with Ralph in the museums and "narrow and sombre Florentine streets" (I, 354), where he acts as "cicerone to his eager young kinswoman" (I, 353) seem a parallel preparation for Madame Merle's taking Isabel to visit Osmond's "view, his pictures, his daughter" (I, 359). Ralph is led by the prospect of this visit to speak "with more apparent earnestness than he commonly used" (I, 360) as he declares Madame Merle "too good, too kind, too clever, too learned, too accomplished, too everything. She's too complete, in a word" (I, 361). Isabel's rebuking Ralph for his mistrust of Madame Merle by again calling him "odious," brings back her earlier use of the word at Gardencourt, where his slighter warning has quickened her response to the "cleverest woman in the world." Here again he simply makes her more eager for the visit to the villa, where she first becomes really interested in Osmond as the owner of "his pictures, his medallions and tapestries" (I, 375), which Ralph's tutelage has prepared her to appreciate. It is when the "deep appeal of Rome" (I, 413) has fully kindled her imagination that Osmond again appears; and her ecstasy over the city is mingled with the ecstasy of falling in love. Her "strange elation" (I, 419) is response to both; and the comedy of her confusing the city and the man as the climax of European civilization is fraught with portents of tragedy.

For Ralph the irony is very cruel comedy. In the heartrending scene in the garden of the Palazzo Crescentini, where he finally speaks his anguished warning to Isabel against Osmond, the sense of his suffering is increased by the description of the place: "A sweeter spot at this moment could not have been imagined. The stillness of noontide hung over it, and the warm shade, enclosed and still, made bowers like spacious caves. Ralph was sitting there in the clear gloom, at the base of a statue of Terpsichore—a dancing nymph with taper fingers and inflated draperies in the manner of Bernini" (II, 63). It is Isabel's still ludicrous folly which causes his pain. In this Italian

garden, all that Europe has so far meant to her comes out in her majestic declaration that Osmond's mind "is the finest I know" (II, 69). Even the irony of her rejoicing that Mr. Touchett has put it in her power to marry a poor man is less poignant than her chiding Ralph for not appreciating Osmond: "You might know a gentleman when you see one—you might know a fine mind" (II, 73). To such a state of delusion her European education has brought her.

Just as the European scene is partly responsible for her delusion, it is used to reflect and reveal her subsequent suffering. The coldness of the Palazzo Roccanera is like the mask of "fixed and mechanical" (II, 142) serenity which Isabel as fine lady shows to the world on her grand Thursday evenings. Isabel, as actually as Pansy, is "immured in a kind of domestic fortress" (II, 100). Her drives in the campagna are her chief solace: "She had long before this taken old Rome into her confidence, for in a world of ruins the ruin of her happiness seemed a less unnatural catastrophe. . . . Small it was, in the large Roman record, and her haunting sense of the continuity of the human lot easily carried her from the less to the greater. She had become deeply, tenderly acquainted with Rome; it interfused and moderated her passion. But she had grown to think of it chiefly as the place where people had suffered" (II, 327-28). What makes this self-identification more pitiful is its recalling Isabel's first ecstatic response to Rome in the time when "she would even have been willing to take these hours for the happiest she was ever to know. The sense of the terrible human past was heavy to her, but that of something altogether contemporary would suddenly give it wings that it could wave in the blue" (I, 413). Thus James uses Europe and the Europeanized characters operating on Isabel as one of the ways of showing her tragic suffering as the result of her comic folly.

The satire by which the tragic evil in the novel is defined is, of course, inextricably interwoven with the

European theme and the doubleness of its handling. The essence of the many-shaded irony in the treatment of Madame Merle is in Ralph's conversation with Isabel. He reiterates his mother's point of her value in educating Isabel; but he implies a much less single judgment of the value itself:

"She 's a capital person for you to know. Since you wish to see the world you could n't have a better guide."

"I suppose you mean by that that she 's worldly?"

"Worldly? No," said Ralph, "she 's the great round world itself!" (I, 362).

Ralph, for all his penetration into her character, feels sorry for her: "She had got herself into perfect training, but she had won none of the prizes. She was always plain Madame Merle, the widow of a Swiss *négociant,* with a small income and a large acquaintance, who stayed with people a great deal and was almost as universally 'liked' as some new volume of smooth twaddle. The contrast between this position and any one of some half-dozen others that he supposed to have at various moments engaged her hope had an element of the tragical" (I, 363). It is an indication of the distance James has come since the portrayal of the de Bellegardes first as objects of exaggerated satire and then suddenly as melodramatic villains that he leads the reader and Isabel herself into pity for "Poor, poor Madame Merle" (II, 331), who at length indicts both Osmond and herself by saying to him, "You have made me as bad as yourself" (II, 335). After Osmond has left her, she looks abstractedly at the delicate cup in which Osmond has found a crack. " 'Have I been so vile all for nothing?' she vaguely wailed" (II, 338).

There is bitter comedy in the trick played by fate on Madame Merle; and James brings even the appalling Osmond into the orbit of this kind of terrible laughter. For him too there is bewilderment and frustration in finding that he has got a wife who cannot conform to his rigid system of propriety. "The real offense, as [Isabel] ultimate-

ly perceived, was her having a mind of her own at all. . . .
He had plenty of contempt, and it was proper his wife
should be as well furnished; but that she should turn the
hot light of her disdain upon his own conception of things—
this was a danger he had not allowed for" (II, 200-201).
Part of the concentration of the effect of Isabel's night-
long vigil in which she realizes the full evil of Osmond's
monstrous egotism and of his hatred of her comes from the
fact that she also realizes "the magnitude of *his* deception"
(II, 194) and that when he had told her before their marriage "that she had too many ideas and that she must get
rid of them . . . What he had meant had been the whole
thing—her character, the way she felt, the way she judged.
This was what she had kept in reserve; this was what he
had not known until he had found himself—with the door
closed behind, as it were—set down face to face with it.
She had a certain way of looking at life which he took
as a personal offence" (II, 194-95). Thus in the agonized
scrutiny initiated by Isabel's beginning to discover the full
duplicity practised against her, she also lays bare the extent to which Osmond himself has been duped.

The use of Isabel as an instrument of satire from
her earliest encounter with Osmond makes James's mockery
of him peculiarly penetrating and intensifies its relation
to the tragedy. It is through Isabel's pondering Osmond's
behavior exactly while she is in the process of falling in
love with him that James reveals him not only as the
"sterile dilletante" (II, 71) Ralph calls him, but as a crassly
vulgar man. It is after the bad taste of Osmond's remarks
about his sister's private life that Isabel incongruously
decides that "she had never met a person of so fine a grain"
(I, 376); and the proofs she gives herself make us pity her
even as we laugh at her underlining of Osmond's morbid
self-absorption. "His sensibility had governed him—possibly governed him too much; it had made him impatient
of vulgar troubles and had led him to live by himself, in
a sorted, sifted, arranged world, thinking about art and

beauty and history. He had consulted his taste in everything—his taste alone perhaps, as a sick man consciously
incurable consults at last only his lawyer: that was what
made him so different from everyone else. Ralph had
something of this same quality, this appearance of thinking
that life was a matter of connoisseurship; but in Ralph it
was an anomaly, a kind of humorous excrescence, whereas
in Mr. Osmond it was the keynote, and everything was in
harmony with it" (I, 376-77). In spite of her mistaken
awe, she does retain common sense enough to wonder why
he has asked her what she thought of the Countess Gemini:
"it was a little singular he should sacrifice his fraternal
feeling to his curiosity" (I, 378). She listens with reverence
and with unusual care to make the right responses while
he lectures about the treasures of his collection: "His kindness almost surprised our young friend, who wondered why
he should take so much trouble for her; and she was op-
pressed at last with the accumulation of beauty and knowledge to which she found herself introduced" (I, 378).
Again in the midst of his flagrant display of complacency
about his plan of life, "to be as quiet as possible . . . Not
to worry—not to strive nor struggle. To resign myself. To
be content with little" (I, 381), and the superficially self-
depreciating boast, "I was simply the most fastidious young
gentleman living" (I, 382), Isabel puzzles over his having
"the conscious air of a man who has brought himself to
confess something. . . . Why should a man who struck her
as having a great fund of reserve suddenly bring himself
to be so confidential?" (I, 381). The whole of Isabel's in-
ward musing during the scene is one of the funniest examples of the confusion of her intelligence by ignorance
and innocence, by the fact that: "Her mind contained no
class offering a natural place to Mr. Osmond" (I, 376). But
the comedy of her misjudgment is an enforcement of the
sharper comedy in the satire of Osmond and at the same
time gives a premonition of the tragic consequences of her
error.

James follows so far as it suits his artistic purpose the advice to himself, imagined in the Preface, to keep the focus on the heroine as center of consciousness and "to press least hard . . . on the consciousness of your heroine's satellites, especially the male" (*The Art of the Novel*, p. 51). But he gives appreciable scope to the consciousness of Ralph and by doing so intensifies the fusion of tragedy and comedy. Ralph is introduced with affection: "Tall, lean, loosely and feebly put together, he had an ugly, sickly, witty, charming face. . . . He looked clever and ill" (I, 5). The tone of his jesting with his father in the opening scene of the novel reveals both his wit and the depth of his affection; and his immediate enjoyment of Isabel shows his responsiveness to impressions. James thus conveys his charm before pointing out the qualities which make him one of the most appealing of Jamesian observers. "His outward conformity to the manners that surrounded him was none the less the mask of a mind that greatly enjoyed its independence, on which nothing long imposed itself, and which, naturally inclined to adventure and irony, indulged in a boundless liberty of appreciation" (I, 49). He indulges the inclination to irony most freely at his own expense since it is only by self-mockery that he makes bearable the illness which condemns him to a spectator's place in life. " 'When people forget I 'm a poor creature I 'm often incommoded," he said. 'But it 's worse when they remember it!' " (I, 214). He has already told Isabel "I keep a band of music in my ante-room. . . . It has orders to play without stopping; it renders me two excellent services. It keeps the sounds of the world from reaching the private apartments, and it makes the world think that dancing 's going on within" (I, 82). His wit plays over everything and is a large element in the tone of the whole English section of the novel, as he "chaffs" his cousin and, by his supposed refusal to take life seriously, leads Henrietta into the most extravagantly earnest defenses of American earnestness.

It is his "boundless liberty of appreciation" which makes him contribute to the impression that Isabel is "a really interesting little figure." His finding her "entertainment of a high order" (I, 86) makes her more entertaining. " 'A character like that' he said to himself—'a real little passionate force to see at play is the finest thing in nature.' . . . Isabel's originality was that she gave one an impression of having intentions of her own. 'Whenever she executes them,' said Ralph, 'may I be there to see!' " (I, 86-87). But his sense of irony colors even his joy in Isabel, and his appreciation of her vitality does not obscure the clarity of his insight into her faults. In the quiet conversation with her in Winchester Square, he points out to her with unironic candor: "As a fact you think nothing in the world too perfect for you. . . . you 're extremely interesting to yourself" (I, 210-11). The retaining in this serious conversation of some of the feeling of earlier banter makes possible the utterance of the keen judgments that Isabel is to ponder soberly. It is one of the ironies that she attends to Ralph's criticisms of herself and ignores his mistrust of Madame Merle and Osmond; but it is also part of the ironic truth of her nature that her attention to Ralph's criticism is simply another sign of the interest in herself which he has pointed out.

With all his insight, Ralph's judgment is not infallible. James creates him in accordance with what he was to say of Rowland: that the observing center must be acute, but also "bedimmed and befooled and bewildered, anxious, restless, fallible" (*The Art of the Novel*, p. 16). It is Ralph's own imagination, as his father warmly declares, which makes him want Isabel to be able to fulfill the requirements of her imagination. Thus his generous error of judgment in conveying to her half of his own fortune supplies what Madame Merle (thinking of Osmond) has told Isabel is the one thing lacking to make her a *parti*. The rapturous gesture with which Madame Merle betrays her interest in Mrs. Touchett's news that

Isabel is an heiress gives notice—but only to the reader—
that she now considers her young friend an adequate prey
to pursue for Osmond. So the crucial irony of the plot,
which precipitates the whole train of subsequent ironies,
springs with perfect appropriateness from the high imagination of Ralph, who, wanting to put wind in Isabel's
sails, causes her to be put in a cage.

It is, however, her own errors of judgment which
allow her to be caught; and just as she is the center of
interest in the whole novel, it is especially in the presentation of her mistakes that James shows comedy and tragedy
as one. The initial impression of Isabel is predominantly
comic. There is little in the charming scene in which she
captivates all the gentlemen on the lawn at Gardencourt,
and even the "rowdyish terrier" (I, 16), to indicate that
James is launching more than social comedy. But the
whole movement of the conversation leads to Isabel's
declaration, "I 'm very fond of my liberty" (I, 24). This
announcement later seems to have been the promise both
of her folly and of the largeness of being which makes her
suffering tragic. The Albany chapters are more broadly
comic. The picture of the romantic Isabel sitting in the
gloomy "office" trying to fix her mind on a history of
German Thought is interrupted by "our crazy Aunt
Lydia" (I, 32), who makes her eccentricity "a matter of
high but easy irony, or comedy" (I, 36). James reveals the
interest in Isabel's own character in her finding her aunt
"a figure essentially—almost the first she had ever met"
(I, 35). Similarly, the farcical scene in which the Ludlows
take opposing views of Isabel's superiority conveys the
feeling both that she actually is superior and that she feels
too much "that people were right when they treated her
as if she were rather superior" (I, 67). This sentence comes
from the second of the passages of extended analysis near
the beginning of the novel and is a good example of their
comic tone, which laughs at Isabel's naïveté with an affection plainly showing that she is to be taken seriously. The

condescension in "the poor girl liked to be thought clever, but she hated to be thought bookish" evaporates in the next sentence: "she had an immense curiosity about life and was constantly staring and wondering" (I, 45). James shows at once her high mindedness and her folly: "The girl had a certain nobleness of imagination which rendered her a good many services and played her a great many tricks" (I, 68). He is more explicit than he usually allows himself to be in announcing his intention in her portrayal: "Altogether, with her meagre knowledge, her inflated ideals, her confidence at once innocent and dogmatic, her temper at once exacting and indulgent, her mixture of curiosity and fastidiousness, of vivacity and indifference, her desire to look very well and to be if possible even better, her determination to see, to try, to know, her combination of the delicate, desultory, flame-like spirit and the eager and personal creature of conditions: she would be an easy victim of scientific criticism if she were not intended to awaken on the reader's part an impulse more tender and more purely expectant" (I, 69).[7] Comedy and tragedy are even more overtly connected in the passage where James directly addresses the reader: "Smile not, however, I venture to repeat, at this simple young woman from Albany who debated whether she should accept an English peer before he had offered himself and who was disposed to believe that on the whole she could do better. She was a person of great good faith, and if there was a great deal of folly in her wisdom those who judge her severely may have the satisfaction of finding that, later, she became consistently wise only at the cost of an amount of

7. The traits given to Isabel and the tone of indulgent laughter here and in much of the comedy of her romanticism suggest that James is using a created character to whom he gives autonomous life partly as a means of looking at his own youth and at youthful idealism itself, somewhat as Johnson used Rasselas. There is a comprehensive survey of suggestions of actual models for Isabel by Oscar Cargill, "'The Portrait of a Lady': A Critical Reappraisal," *Modern Fiction Studies*, III (Spring, 1957), 11-18, reprinted in *The Novels of Henry James* (New York, 1961), pp. 79-86.

folly which will constitute almost a direct appeal to charity"
(I, 144-45).

James's attitude of mingled detachment and involvement, of comedy and tragedy, apparent in all these passages
of comment, is equally apparent in the dramatic rendering of Isabel's character. It may be said in general that
she is comic up to the time of her marriage and tragic
thereafter; but there is no abrupt break, such as occurs in
The American, because tragedy is interfused in the comedy
of the early part of the novel. All three proposal scenes
illustrate the flicker of comedy over what is essentially
serious and holds tragic possibilities. Lord Warburton's
ends:

> "There's one thing more," he went on. "You know,
> if you don't like Lockleigh—if you think it's damp
> or anything of that sort—you need never go within
> fifty miles of it. It's not damp, by the way; I've had
> the house thoroughly examined; it's perfectly safe
> and right. But if you should n't fancy it you need n't
> dream of living in it. There's no difficulty whatever
> about that; there are plenty of houses. I thought
> I'd just mention it; some people don't like a moat,
> you know. Good-bye."
> "I adore a moat," said Isabel. "Good-bye"
> (I, 154-55).

The cruder clash of the meeting with Goodwood in London gives a rough edge to the dialogue:

> "Henrietta's certainly not a model of all the deli-
> cacies!" she exclaimed with bitterness. "It was a
> great liberty to take."
> "I suppose I'm not a model either—of those
> virtues or of any others. The fault's mine as much
> as hers."
> As Isabel looked at him it seemed to her that
> his jaw had never been more square. This might
> have displeased her, but she took a different turn.
> "No, it's not your fault so much as hers. What
> you 've done was inevitable, I suppose, for *you*" (I,
> 217).

But in spite of the difference of her reaction to the two men, it is as a threat to her "personal independence" (I, 228) that she rejects Goodwood, just as she could not marry Lord Warburton because "the idea failed to support any enlightened prejudice in favour of the free exploration of life that she had hitherto entertained or was now capable of entertaining" (I, 155). With Goodwood her greater frankness lays her more open to the smile at her folly which James has deprecated. Her declaration, "I wish to choose my fate," (I, 229) is at once ludicrously naïve and portentous of the suffering that James has promised. When Henrietta, dismayed at her rejection of Goodwood, warns her, "You're drifting to some great mistake" (I, 235), her own earnestness is comical; but her concern for Isabel is justified.

By the time of the third proposal, Isabel has already made the "great mistake" of falling in love with Osmond; and James has made fully clear the tragic implications behind the comedy. The proposal scene, like the earlier ones between Isabel and Osmond, is presented with laughter at them both; but the laughter deepens mistrust of Osmond and apprehension for Isabel. He finds her sitting "alone in a wilderness of yellow upholstery. . . . For Osmond the place was ugly to distress; the false colours, the sham splendour were like vulgar, bragging, lying talk" (II, 13). He spouts as egotistically as he has during Isabel's visit to his villa and produces a still more worshipful response in her. She says solemnly:

"It would n't be remarkable if you did think it ridiculous that I should have the means to travel when you 've not; for you know everything, and I know nothing."

"The more reason why you should travel and learn," smiled Osmond. "Besides," he added as if it were a point to be made, "I don't know everything."

Isabel was not struck with the oddity of his saying this gravely (II, 15-16).

This double satire continues through the conversation to his declaration:

"What I wish to say to you . . . is that I find I 'm in love with you" (II, 17),

and to the ominous interchange:

". . . you 'll discover what a worship I have for propriety."

"You 're not conventional?" Isabel gravely asked.

"I like the way you utter that word! No, I'm not conventional: I'm convention itself" (II, 21).

The increasing momentum of tragic implication in the comedy of the three proposal scenes is representative of the way James uses comedy throughout the first half of the novel to build up a pressure of apprehension for Isabel which makes her suffering, when it finally begins, seem all the more overpowering. When Isabel reappears after her marriage, she has already learned much of the wisdom which James has promised that she will discover through folly; she is no longer treated comically, though she can be the instrument of bitter comedy. Both her unhappiness and her management of it are revealed in her conversation with Lord Warburton when he appears at one of her Thursdays:

"Well now, I suppose you're very happy and all that sort of thing?"

Isabel answered with a quick laugh; the tone of his remark struck her almost as the accent of comedy. "Do you suppose if I were not I 'd tell you?"

"Well, I don't know. I don't see why not."

"I do then. Fortunately, however, I'm very happy."

"You 've got an awfully good house."

"Yes, it 's very pleasant. But that's not my merit—it 's my husband's."

"You mean he has arranged it?"

"Yes, it was nothing when we came."

"He must be very clever."

"He has a genius for upholstery," said Isabel (II, 131).

Her own reference to her life as comedy betrays a kind of irony of which the younger Isabel would have been totally incapable. When she is trying to get her friends out of Rome, she tells Henrietta:

"I want to be alone, . . ."
"You won't be that so long as you've so much company at home."
"Ah, they 're part of the comedy. You others are spectators."
"Do you call it a comedy, Isabel Archer?" Henrietta rather grimly asked.
"The tragedy then if you like. You 're all looking at me; it makes me uncomfortable" (II, 303).

In the last part of the novel there are still characters like Rosier and the Countess who are pathetic in their power to suffer at the same time that they are comic butts; Isabel, however, is no longer one of them. Perhaps Erasmus's Folly, looking out from the brink of heaven and smiling at holding all mortals under her sway, can laugh at Isabel still. But for fellow mortals her very folly has made her now a richly tragic character.

The progress of her suffering is the progress of her tragic enlightenment about her own folly quite as much as it is increasing discovery of the baseness surrounding her. How much of the old Isabel survives is revealed in the conversation in which she tells Henrietta that she cannot publish her mistake: "I don't know what great unhappiness might bring me to; but it seems to me I shall always be ashamed. One must accept one's deeds. I married him before all the world; I was perfectly free; it was impossible to do anything more deliberate. One can't change that way" (II, 284). After the Countess has enlightened her about Osmond's relation to Madame Merle, when "it seemed to her that only now she fully measured the great undertaking of matrimony" (II, 360-61), she suffers in

exactly the way most relevant to her young innocence and
idealism in the first part of the novel. "What he thought
of her she knew, what he was capable of saying to her she
had felt; yet they were married, for all that, and marriage
meant that a woman should cleave to the man with whom,
uttering tremendous vows, she had stood at the altar"
(II, 361). Even in the final meeting with Ralph, she "felt
a passionate need to cry out and accuse herself" (II, 414).
Ralph leads her beyond self-accusation, however, and this
scene approaches comedy in Dante's sense of beatitude in
the discovery that there is something deeper than pain, that
"love remains" (II, 416).

But James does not end the novel in this mood of
peace. The rightness of "the conclusion in which nothing
is concluded" will probably continue to be debated by
critics. It has at any rate an ambiguity which James has
plainly promised by the whole treatment of Isabel and
made explicit in the contradictions of her thought during
the journey from Rome.

> Deep in her soul—deeper than any appetite for re-
> nunciation—was the sense that life would be her
> business for a long time to come. And at moments
> there was something inspiring, almost enlivening,
> in the conviction. It was a proof of strength—it
> was a proof she should some day be happy again.
> It could n't be she was to live only to suffer; she
> was still young, after all, and a great many things
> might happen to her yet. To live only to suffer—
> only to feel the injury of life repeated and enlarged
> —it seemed to her she was too valuable, too capable,
> for that. . . . but Isabel recognized, as it passed be-
> fore her eyes, the quick vague shadow of a long
> future. She should never escape; she should last to
> the end. Then the middle years wrapped her about
> again and the grey curtain of her indifference closed
> her in (II, 392-93).

This attempt to look into her future parallels the agonized
reflection on her past in the midnight vigil in Rome; but

she cannot reach such clear judgment on what is still to come.

Isabel's going back to Rome, which is both a flight from Goodwood's passion and a return to what she regards as her duty, is appropriate to the feeling of mingled motives which have made her convincingly lifelike (and thus both comic and tragic) from the beginning of the novel. Furthermore, while rounding out an artistic movement of action, it gives the feeling that the continuity of life extends beyond the limits of the novel. In *The Portrait of a Lady*, James has solved the problem of the novelist which he states in the Preface to *Roderick Hudson:* "He is in the perpetual predicament that the continuity of things is the whole matter, for him, of comedy and tragedy; that this continuity is never, by the space of an instant or an inch, broken, and that, to do anything at all, he has at once intensely to consult and intensely to ignore it" (*The Art of the Novel*, p. 5).

The Portrait of a Lady marks the culmination of the first period of James's mature development and shows him in full command of his artistic powers. As he went on to write other sorts of novels in other manners, he continued to the end of his career to present the mingled tragedy and comedy of life through the means which are brought together here: the juxtaposition of opposing cultures, the use of satire to define evil, the portrayal of minor characters who are both ridiculous and pathetic, and the concentration of tragedy and comedy in the centers of consciousness whether of observer or of principal character. His fictions can be experienced only as artistic wholes; but it should enhance that experience to examine separately the elements in James's rendering of the tragic comedy of life as they appear in a range of examples throughout the body of his work. Such an examination is the object of the chapters which follow.

III ~ International Tragedy and Comedy

The principle of contrast was for James of the essence of artistic interest; and he found a source of contrast regularly in what he calls the "mixture of manners." He uses the phrase repeatedly in the Preface to the "Lady Barbarina" volume of international tales, where he explains that the mixture he most frequently depicts is international because "one never really chooses one's general range of vision—the experience from which ideas and themes and suggestions spring: . . . The subject thus pressed upon the artist is the necessity of his case and the fruit of his consciousness; . . . The artist . . . has but to have his honest sense of life to find it fed at every pore even as the birds of the air are fed" (*The Art of the Novel*, p. 201). In the Preface to the *Daisy Miller* volume James elaborates on the reasons for the predominance of the international theme in his fiction and lists the works which he says almost exhaust the number of his "more or less sustained things" in which it does *not* appear (*The Art of the Novel*, pp. 280-81). It is strikingly true of most of these works, as well as of *The Bostonians*, which he does not list, that

the drama still arises from the mixture of manners, the encounter of characters who come together bringing from different social groups or classes different sets of preconceived attitudes and habits of behavior in addition to and complicating individual differences of temperament. The juxtaposing of contrasting, often conflicting, limitations of background, whether the contrast is international or not, is one of James's favorite ways of revealing both the tragedy and the comedy of life, and usually both at once. The collision of cultures in his international fiction is always dramatic; but there is great variety in the ways tragedy and comedy enhance each other in the dramas thus produced. "The Pension Beaurepas," *The Reverberator,* and *The Golden Bowl,* three works of different lengths and different periods, suggest the range of ways in which he shows the international theme as both tragic and comic.

In "The Pension Beaurepas," as in "A Bundle of Letters" and "The Point of View," which he groups with it in the "Lady Barbarina" volume of the New York Edition, James is bringing together disparate attitudes by a frankly acknowledged device. In this case he manages by means of the assemblage in a pension after the model of Balzac in *Père Goriot,* to which he lets the narrator call attention. He does not, however, follow Balzac in giving himself length of narration in which to develop his varied characters, and consequently he relies rather obtrusively on the narrator to give interpretation and to direct response. He even calls attention to his own presentation of types by having Madame Beaurepas repeatedly judge her guests by classifications; and the chief function of M. Pigeonneau, the only European guest who is named, is to apply his categories of sexual charm to the ladies. Yet this very emphasis on the typicality of the characters gives them substance; and the combined comedy and tragedy they enact gains power as a reflection of what might be seen in any Swiss pension frequented by Americans.

The comedy with which Mrs. Church is handled is

wholly satiric. She belongs to the type Madame Beaurepas knows well, and always finds "deplacé," of impoverished boarders who give themselves airs. "Yet there are people who, the less they pay, take themselves the more au sérieux. My most difficult boarders have always been those who 've fiercely bargained and had the cheapest rooms" (*Lady Barbarina,* etc., p. 395). It is again Madame Beaurepas who announces the other classification to which Mrs. Church belongs: "c'est une de ces mamans, comme vous en avez, qui promènent leur fille" (p. 436). But once she is firmly placed in these broad categories, James can proceed to the farcical scenes in which she displays her particular pose of being at once ladylike and learned. She never raises her voice even when she disputes the fare with her cabman and avoids tipping him by finding that he has left behind the little red bag he should have held between his knees; or when she comes to fetch her daughter whom she discovers consuming an afternoon ice in public in the company only of the reprehensible Miss Ruck and the two male fellow boarders. She is regularly on display in the salon, equipped with her octavo volume in German and arranging the lamp or the furniture preparatory to reading it. She disdains the society of most of the people in the pensions where she has spent her life as much as that in America, which she feels that she still knows well enough to condemn. Her scorn is in itself pathetic as well as ludicrous; but her claim of knowing European homes and having the *entrée* of old Genevese society is still more grotesque. With the economy of caricature, James shows in Mrs. Church the ridiculous gestures of this kind of displaced person.

Except in the scenes with her mother, where she responds with an acquiescence as farcical as her mother's demands for assent, the handling of Aurora is less broad. The impression of her is made ambiguous by the narrator's being half in love with her and yet feeling that Madame Beaurepas is right in finding her sly. He wonders

at the combination in her of submissiveness to her mother and the "mocking freedom" (p. 434) of her tone with him. But one thing which he plainly sees is that she will never be the American girl she aspires to be. Her mother's bringing her up as the monstrosity of a learned *jeune fille* who is "familiar with the results of modern science [and] keeps pace with the new historical school" (p. 430) has unfitted her for any conceivable station; and she is at once funny and pathetic in her attempts to break out of her rôle by misplaced sallies of boldness. Her begging the narrator to tell her when she sounds the wrong note is part of her coquettish attempt to ensnare him as a means of escape to America; but her wiles evoke more pity than scorn. She pursues him as the only young man available; and her recklessly following him into the garden on the night before her mother whisks her off to Dresden to remove her from Miss Ruck's corrupting company seems the behavior of desperation.[1]

With Mrs. Church thwarted in her attempt to get rid of her deplorable compatriots and routed herself from the scene, the narrator can devote the whole attention of his last day in Geneva to the drama of the Rucks. The two families have been steadily used as foils for each other; and the impression of both is conveyed in relation to the background of the Pension Beaurepas. This relation, however, like everything else which concerns them, is different for the two families. Mrs. Church and her daughter are the product of their life in a succession of such pensions. The attempt to become Europeanized is responsible for the particular kinds of fools Mrs. Church has made of herself and her daughter and determines both the comedy and the pathos of their lot. The Rucks—mother, father, and daughter—are all three wholly American products. In presenting them, it is a question of using the European background to isolate and define the traits which have been

1. James develops both her absurdity and her pathos as he lets her record her own later adventures in "The Point of View."

developed in American society. Their very blindness to
what either Mrs. Church or the narrator sees in Europe
underlines the definition of their types. For Sophy and
her mother Geneva is simply an aggregation of jewelers'
shops; for Mr. Ruck, it is equally simply the place he has
reached in carrying out his sentence of transportation.

In portraying Mr. Ruck's "two ladies" in their relentless pursuit of purchasing more and more adornments
for their already bedizened persons, James is as implacably
satiric as in the portrayal of Mrs. Church. Probably
nowhere else does he give a more unmitigated impression
of the American woman's commitment to the duty expressed by the vivacious Mrs. Westgate of "An International Episode": "An American woman who respects
herself . . . must buy something every day of her life"
(p. 317). They have bought so much during their month
in Paris that Mr. Ruck has finally grown "restless" enough
to force them protesting into the coach which bears them
away only to new exploits in the jewelers' shops of Geneva.
The most shocking part of their heartlessness is their unconsciousness of it. Mrs. Ruck wishes vaguely that Mr.
Ruck would get well, but largely because his "restlessness"
confuses her purchasing campaign. Sophy, who prides
herself on always getting what she wants, does not mean to
let him alone until he takes her back to Paris. Meanwhile,
she is simply contemptuous of his feeble remonstrance
about her wanting the blue cross. As she and her mother
go off to look for "a nice little gold chain" (p. 411) on
which she intends to display the cross, he can only utter
what becomes his refrain: "Well, they want to pick up
something, . . . That's the principal interest for ladies"
(p. 412). That his restlessness, of which they complain, is
born of despair over his illness and his approaching bank-
ruptcy, they are as unaware as they are of the scenery,
which they dismiss by saying that they have seen "plenty
of mountains at home" (p. 410).

They are too unconscious to suggest any tragical

possibilities in themselves; but in their effect on Mr. Ruck, they are among James's most sardonic demonstrations of the way in which comic characters create suffering for those of larger capacity. Mr. Ruck is as blindly provincial in his attitude toward Europe as are his two ladies; but he is much more human. Even his provincialism is amiably presented and has an element of friendly jocularity, as when he comments that the small size of the Swiss newspaper suits a small country. When he sits with his back to the view and a newspaper unfolded on his lap, he is the picture of desolation in his imperviousness to his surroundings. Indeed, pity has been rather too obviously demanded for him from the first by the narrator's beginning to feel sorry for him almost immediately after he has consigned him to a type with the reflection: "I had often seen him, or his equivalent, in the hotel-parlours of my native land" (p. 399). As soon as the poor man begins to talk of his early business success and his anxiety over being sent to Europe during the present financial crisis just when he most needs to be on hand to attend to his interests, his personal plight enforces his representation of a type. His drollery remains comic; but his humor and good humor accentuate the helplessness with which he contemplates his ruin. The narrator explains him to Mrs. Church as the type of the "broken-down man of business. He 's broken-down in health and I think he must be broken-down in fortune. He has spent his whole life in buying and selling and watching prices, so that he knows how to do nothing else." But he goes on: "Poor Mr. Ruck, . . . strikes me as a really tragic figure. He 's getting bad news every day from home; his affairs may be going to the dogs. He 's unable, with his lost nerve, to apply himself; so he has to stand and watch his fortunes ebb. He has been used to doing things in a big way and he feels 'mean' if he makes a fuss about bills. So the ladies keep sending them in. . . . So by way of not being mean, of being a good American husband and father, poor Ruck stands staring

at bankruptcy" (pp. 460-61). After the news of bank-ruptcy has come and the narrator has done what he can to give at least company, if not comfort, to the stricken man by taking him to the little *brasserie* so that he will not have to endure a meal at the pension, the walk along the Rue de Rhône brings them inevitably upon the Ruck ladies in the largest and most brilliant of the jewelers' shops. All the cruel irony of the situation is imaged in the final scene of Sophy flaunting the bracelet she has purchased and demanding a satin instead of a velvet case for it while Mrs. Ruck responds to the narrator's whispered "I 'm afraid he 's not at all well" by exclaiming "Well, I must say I wish he 'd improve!" (p. 475). Mr. Ruck, who has been whistling in a low tone, bids goodbye to his friend saying, "Don't wait for me, . . . I 've got to see this thing through" (p. 476). James speaks in the Preface of having wasted the treasures of the "unearthly poetry" (*The Art of the Novel*, p. 216) of his scene in "The Pension Beaurepas." But while he may not have done enough to satisfy himself with the charm of old Geneva, he has made sufficient use of it to bring out devastatingly the relation of comedy to misery in the lives of the inmates of the Pension Beaurepas.

～　　～　　～

The Dossons of *The Reverberator* make a neat parallel to the Rucks as the family of an American business man and his two ladies. They are as completely as are the Rucks the products of the American business world and bring the limitations of American society with them to Europe. Delia and Francie even share the preoccupation with shopping as the "principal interest for ladies," though their purchases stop at handkerchiefs by the hundred which "only makes fifty apiece" (*The Reverberator*, etc., p. 17) instead of jewels. But whereas Europe serves for the Rucks simply to display more vividly what could have

taken place at home, the whole action of *The Reverberator* depends upon the confrontation of American with European failures in perception. Mrs. Ruck and Sophy could have been heartlessly extravagant while Mr. Ruck's health and business collapsed in New York. But Francie Dosson could not have shocked and bewildered any segment of American society as she does the tight little group in the Cours la Rienne and the Place Beauvau.

The Dossons are as devoted a family as the Rucks are divided; and Mr. Dosson has no business worries to qualify his pleasure in paying for expensive entertainment for his "chickens" and their friends. An altogether sunnier atmosphere is created by his serene pleasure in Delia's efficiency and Francie's cultivation (proved by her leaving a trail of Tauchnitz volumes behind her in her progress through the hotels of Europe), by Delia's affectionate bustling of her sister, and by Francie's charming pliancy. The warmth of family feeling promises a happier tale than that of the Rucks. Yet exactly the atmosphere of ingenuous goodness and good intentions generated by these amiable people emphasizes the near approach of the novel to tragedy, for all its happy ending and James's calling it a *jeu d'esprit* (*The Art of the Novel*, p. 180).

The Proberts, whose limitations James juxtaposes to those of the Dossons, are Gallicized Americans, more French than the French. The father "a Carolinian and a Catholic, [is] a Gallomaniac of the old American type," (p. 39) who has married his three daughters to Frenchmen and lost his older son in defense of France in the "Terrible Year," 1870. Gaston, the youngest of this family which "had been so completely Gallicised that the affairs of each member of it were the affairs of all the rest" (p. 40), falls in love with Francie Dosson's beauty the moment he sets eyes on her in the studio of his friend Waterlow. Visual impressions, "things that happened through my eyes" (p. 46), as he tells Waterlow, are the most important in life for Gaston; and he falls in love largely with the "charm of

line" (p. 45) in Francie's modeling. "And think of the
delight of having that charming object before one's eyes—
always, always! It makes a different look-out for life" (p.
78), he says ardently to his sister Mme. de Brécourt, whom
he is trying to win over and whose help he seeks in per-
suading the rest of the family. James's laughter at the boy
is not mocking, but he is quite explicit about Gaston's
having a simplicity equal to Francie's own: "He was in
search of freshness, but he need n't have gone far: he
would have had but to turn his lantern on his own young
breast to find a considerable store of it" (p. 40). He is as
loving a young creature as Francie herself. His friend
Waterlow, who serves the useful purpose of confidant and
interpreter, accuses him of being afraid of his sisters; but
he knows that actually the bond is much more delicate.
"Family feeling among them was not a tyranny but a
religion, and in regard to Mesdames de Brécourt, de
Cliché, and de Douves what Gaston most feared was that
he might seem to them not to love them enough" (p. 69).
When Waterlow suggests that he could marry Francie
whether his family approve or not, his reply is, "One
can't break with one's traditions in an hour" (p. 72). The
tradition to which he most clings is that of fraternal and
filial tenderness; and in the glow of his love for Francie,
he is sure that if he can just get his family to know her,
her own sweetness will guarantee her being taken into
the circle of their affections. James lets him bring off this
feat through Waterlow's help in the comedy of getting
Mme. de Brécourt to commit herself to extravagant admiration first of Waterlow's portrait of Francie and then
of the girl herself before he confesses that he wants to bring
her into the family. After her own horror of having a
sister-in-law who says "Parus" has subsided, she does en-
thusiastically espouse his cause. In the richly comic scenes
of Probert family conclaves and visits in form to the Dossons which she brings about, James seems to be following
the movement of romantic comedy in which young love is

to triumph over the opposition of elders, whose rigidities are gaily satirized.

Young love does eventually triumph, but not before the little drama has come very near to tragedy. The instrument of evil is the egregious Mr. Flack, who is the epitome of all the bold vulgarity which James loathed in "newspaperism," with its crass invasion of privacy. He is the European correspondent of *The Reverberator* and the accepted mentor of the Dossons. "What he mainly made clear to them was that it was really most kind of a young man who had so many big things on his mind to find sympathy for questions, for issues, he used to call them, that could occupy the telegraph and the press so little as theirs. He came every day to set them in the right path, pointing out its charms to them in a way that made them feel how much they had been in the wrong" (p. 26). He has expected to marry Francie himself and thus secure a fortune as well as a charming and docile wife. When in refusing him she offers to get money from "Poppa" for his paper, he cries, " 'Lord, you 're too sweet! . . . Do you suppose I 'd ever touch a cent of your father's money?'—a speech not rankly hypocritical, inasmuch as the young man, who made his own discriminations, had never been guilty, and proposed to himself never to be, of the indelicacy of tugging at his potential father-in-law's purse-strings with his own hand." He goes on arguing with Francie, "assuring her that he had brains, heart and material proofs of a college education" until he brings her to the point of tears; yet when he asks at the end of the scene,

"Will you keep me as a friend?"

"Why Mr. Flack, *of course* I will!" cried the easy creature (pp. 65-67).

This proposal scene is a good example of the way James uses the crassness of Mr. Flack not only to exhibit American vulgarity at its worst, but to define the degree of American deficiency in perception on the part of the Dossons. Francie is not in love with the newspaperman;

but she has no sense of his bad taste. "Francie did n't in the least dislike Mr. Flack. . . . she believed him as 'bright' as her father had originally pronounced him and as any young man she was likely to meet. She had no other measure for distinction in young men but their brightness; she had never been present at any imputation of ability or power that this term did n't seem to cover" (p. 59). Delia, too, respects his abilities, though she steadfastly opposes his suit because she wants to launch Francie in society. As for Mr. Dosson, he "never doubted that George M. Flack was remarkably bright. He represented the newspaper, and the newspaper for this man of genial assumptions represented—well, all other representations whatever. . . . If a big newspaper told you everything there was in the world every morning, that was what a big newspaperman would have to know, and Mr. Dosson had never supposed there was anything left to know when such voices as Mr. Flack's and that of his organ had daily been heard" (pp. 22-23).

It is into this same atmosphere of warm acceptance and admiration that Mr. Flack returns after Francie's engagement to Gaston and just as Gaston is leaving to attend to business affairs in America. Gaston's absence from Paris is necessary to James's business as novelist; but it is hard to believe that the business affairs of his father and his prospective father-in-law will be much helped by the boy's presence in America. Mr. Flack does not renew his former intimacy with the Dosson family; but Gaston's absence enables him to get Francie off alone for a day in the Bois, after a visit to Waterlow's studio to look at her portrait, about which he has promised to write an article for *The Reverberator*. It is a revealing sign of Francie's unawareness that she is pleased both for Waterlow and for herself at the prospect of being praised in a big newspaper. And when he leads her on to talk about all the intimate details of Probert family life which Mme. de Brécourt has shared with her and which she regards as "a beautiful story" (p. 136), she prattles away in all innocence. James conveys with

consummate skill the combination in her of a sense of obligation to help Mr. Flack to a good story because he has been responsible for her first meeting with Gaston at Waterlow's studio and because she has promised to be his friend, with her actual childlike pleasure in having her marriage into the *grand monde* written up.

Mr. Flack's lurid article rattles family skeletons in a way that makes them appear totally other than in Francie's romantic narrative; but when it bursts upon the calm of the group in the Place Beauvau, Francie is as filled with consternation at their outrage as they are horror stricken at her perfidy. The courage with which the usually pliant girl, overwhelmed as she is, meets the family conclave of the Proberts and refuses to deny her responsibility, as Mme. de Brécourt begs her to do, makes the meeting one of James's richly dramatic scenes and demonstrates that there is more to her character than the "still and scattered radiance" (p. 16) which has been the source of her charm. One way in which this new strength is made credible is the persistent realism with which Francie has perceived that she is different from the Proberts and will eventually do something to shock them. Before Gaston's proposal, when Delia is praising him as a prince beside Mr. Flack and proclaiming the social station of his sisters, Francie asks: "What good will they do me? . . . They 'll hate me. Before they could turn round I should do something—in perfect innocence—that they 'd think monstrous" (p. 56). Even after she is engaged, she is sure "it will never come off. . . . I 'll be sure to do something" (p. 89). And she finally tells Gaston that she will not visit his sisters before she is safely married because in spite of her present intimacy with Mme. de Brécourt, "in close quarters she might do something that would make them all despise her (p. 115). When she receives Mme. de Brécourt's note summoning her to the family council, she declares fatalistically, "It 's for something bad—something bad" (p. 140), and her only defense against the accusations of the Proberts is,

"I told Gaston I 'd certainly do something you would n't like" (p. 152). As her agitation grows, " 'I *did*—I did tell him so!' Francie repeated with all her fevered candour, alluding to her statement of a moment before and speaking as if she thought the circumstances detracted from the offence" (p. 153). When she goes home to Delia's wrath against the Proberts and Mr. Flack alike and to Mr. Dosson's futile attempts at comfort, what she says is: "Did I ever tell you anything else—did I ever believe in it for an hour?" (p. 157). She declares that she is the one who will suffer most, and she finally collapses and allows Delia to keep her in bed; but she faces the truth as she sees it: "he 'll give me up as he took me. He 'd never have asked me to marry him if he had n't been able to get *them* to accept me: he thinks everything in life of *them*. If they cast me off now he 'll do just the same. He 'll have to choose between us, and when it comes to that he 'll never choose me" (p. 163).

Francie's new dignity is especially apparent in the scene with the outrageous Mr. Flack, who returns at Mr. Dosson's summons thinking he has now achieved Francie's repudiation by the Proberts and can renew his own advances. She asks him quietly about his motives for what he has done; makes plain just how far he has taken advantage of her consenting to talk to him: "You put in things I never said. It seems to me it was very different" (p. 185); and dismisses him: "So we 're square, are n't we? . . . I don't think you ought to ask for anything more. Good-bye" (p. 188).

She betrays more agitation in her interview with Gaston; but she speaks to him with a high lucidity born of her suffering. She insists that the gravity of her offense to the Proberts means that Gaston will have to choose between her and his family; and it is consistent with her fatalistic view that "it will never come off" (p. 89) that she is sure he will choose his family: "You know you did n't come here to tell me that you 're ready to give them up"

(p. 200). Gaston is childish enough to assume that he can bring his family round; but Francie never for a moment entertains such a hope. When he begs her to explain to his family that what she has done was all for him, her answer is: "Never, never! . . . I 've wronged them, and nothing will ever be the same again. It was fatal. If I felt as they do I too would loathe the person who should have done such a thing. It does n't seem to me so bad—the thing in the paper; but you know best. You must go back to them. You know best" (p. 199). She approaches tragic stature when she dismisses her lover, saying: "We 're too terribly different. Everything makes you so. You *can't* give them up—ever, ever. Good-bye—good-bye! That 's all I wanted to tell you" (pp. 200-201).

Yet this scene of tragic renunciation has its element of comedy in Gaston's fatuous assumption that he can reconcile Francie and his family even while he betrays that he shares their consternation over the publishing of "that filthy rubbish" (p. 197). Comedy takes over completely as Gaston paces the floor of Waterlow's studio the next day, pouring out his "torment of hesitation" (p. 204), and finally sees the truth of what Waterlow tells him: that his very survival as an individual depends on his asserting his independence from his family. "She 's the sweetest young thing I ever saw; but even if she happened not to be I should still urge you to marry her, in simple self-preservation" (p. 205). The novel ends with the happy scene at the hotel de L'Univers et de Cheltenham, where Gaston reappears among the packed luggage of the Dossons at ten o'clock in the evening of the same day, announcing jubilantly to Francie, "I 've chosen—I 've chosen," and then to Mr. Dosson, "You must take me with you if you 're going away" (pp. 207-8). It is the kind of romantic happy ending which James does not often permit himself; and since the young people involved are generous and loving, it is perhaps legitimate to add the proper winding up of a fairy tale: "And they lived happily ever after." But the

relief of the happy ending is increased by the impression of how nearly disastrous have been Francie's unawareness of European sensibilities and the Proberts' imperviousness to the appeal of her American innocence.

~ ~ ~

In the Preface to the "Lady Barbarina" volume of international tales, James distinguishes his works which depend on international differences from those which have another "proper subject" and in which the international differences are "quite secondary": "the subject of 'The Wings of the Dove,' or that of 'The Golden Bowl,' has not been the exhibited behavior of certain Americans as Americans, of certain English persons as English, of certain Romans as Romans." He acknowledges that the contrast of Americans and Europeans is obvious and contributive, but declares that "the subject could in each case have been perfectly expressed had *all* the persons concerned been only American or only English or only Roman or whatever" (*The Art of the Novel*, pp. 198-99). The fact that the essential subject of *The Golden Bowl* is something more profoundly human than international differences makes all the more interesting James's use of them in this novel where comedy and tragedy are perhaps more deeply interfused than anywhere else in his fiction.[2]

The imagery of buying and selling which pervades the novel suffuses it with an atmosphere of American

2. It seems relevant that he originally projected the novel as a "short tale" and later considered doing it in response to Henry Harper's request for something short and "intensely international" [*The Notebooks of Henry James*, ed. F. O. Matthiessen and Kenneth B. Murdock (New York, 1947), pp. 131, 188]. Leo B. Levy considers that James escapes melodrama in *The Golden Bowl*, "where the intention (sometimes discernible in earlier works) of bringing the American sensibility into a living, significant union with Europe is fulfilled" [*Versions of Melodrama, University of California Publications in English*, No. 16 (Berkeley, 1957), p. 28].

business values. Indeed, the word "value" itself constantly recurs; and however aesthetic, cultural, or even spiritual, its meaning is in a given instance, it regularly suggests that the value commented on can be purchased for some kind of price. One of the most disturbing parts of the novel is the innocence with which Maggie and her father buy their spouses. Adam's speaking "at his ease" makes more shocking his saying of Charlotte that "she only wants to know what *we* want. Which is what we got her for!" (*The Golden Bowl*, II, 94). In the very opening chapter of the novel Maggie, in all the joyful assurance of first love, jests with the Prince about his being the prize piece of her father's collection. He translates her calling him "an object of price" into the plainer meaning "I cost a lot of money" (I, 12), and they go on to discuss his value.

James makes this traffic in persons without any awareness of wrongdoing on the part of the purchasers seem peculiarly American by linking it thus early in the novel with Mr. Verver's buying up European art treasures to adorn his museum in American City. His acquiring them by his "easy way with his millions" (I, 5) is judged in the images of "spoils" (I, 19) and "rifl[ing]" (I, 141) which surround the accounts of his purchases. The whole conception of the crudity of American City, to which Mr. Verver thinks he can transplant European culture by transporting the spoils he has taken, hovers grotesquely in the background until its final use in Charlotte's banishment. The distant place of exile is present in the novel in somewhat the same way that Mrs. Newsome, with all her Woollett pressure, is present in the Paris of *The Ambassadors*. The fact that Mr. Verver is actually "one of the great collectors of the world" (I, 100), who chooses his pieces with sound aesthetic judgment, makes all the more fatuous his plan which he sees as having "all the sanctions of civilisation; it was positively civilisation condensed, concrete, consummate, set down by his hands as a house on a rock" (I, 145). The folly of his notion that he can

release American City from "the bondage of ugliness" by his "palace of art" (I, 145) is treated comically; but the sinister power to gather spoils by the conquest of sheer wealth shows steadily through the comedy.

The enterprise of acquiring pieces for the museum colors the transactions by which the Ververs acquire *"sposi."* But the *sposi* too are parties to the bargains. And just as the attitude of the Ververs that whatever they want can properly be bought seems peculiarly American, so the attitude of Prince Amerigo and Charlotte that marriage is a legitimate way to recoup one's fortunes seems peculiarly European. Both are paid, or expect to be paid, in other ways besides money; but both are as glad to have Mr. Verver's millions as are the sellers of his art treasures, "great people all over Europe . . . high personages [who] made up to him as the one man on the short authentic list likely to give the price" (I, 100). Both clearly see their marriages as bargains in which they are to be paid for value received. His bargain makes the subject of the Princes's meditation in the opening chapter.

> He was intelligent enough to feel quite humble, to wish not to be in the least hard or voracious, not to insist on his own side of the bargain, to warn himself in short against arrogance and greed. Odd enough, of a truth, was his sense of this last danger—which may illustrate moreover his general attitude toward dangers from within. Personally, he considered, he had n't the vices in question—and that was so much to the good. His race, on the other hand, had had them handsomely enough, and he was somehow full of his race. Its presence in him was like the consciousness of some inexpugnable scent in which his clothes, his whole person, his hands and the hair of his head, might have been steeped as in some chemical bath: the effect was nowhere in particular, yet he constantly felt himself at the mercy of the cause (I, 16).

Charlotte, of course, does not have the Prince's formidable inheritance of race; but she has been born in Florence of

parents already expatriate, and the Prince feels her to be more polyglot than himself. She accepts quite as much as he does the European attitude toward the uses of marriage. She frankly discusses his proposal as a bargain with Mr. Verver himself, acknowledging that she does not "want to be a horrible English old-maid," but that she thinks she "might get what [she] want[s] for less" (I, 219-20). Adam is equally candid about his wanting to have a wife for Maggie's sake so that Charlotte insists on having Maggie's explicit approval. The entire interchange moves in images of buying and selling. Mr. Verver's reflection: "There was after all a hint of offence to a man of his age in being taken, as they said at the shops, on approval" (I, 229), shows the ludicrousness of the whole episode; but it also suggests the possibility of misery in a marriage so contracted.

The marriages on which the plot depends are thus made possible by the bringing together of limitations of attitude which are characteristically, though certainly not exclusively, American on the one hand and European on the other. There is nothing peculiarly American, however, about Maggie's devotion to her father and her husband which creates the movement of the action and the "proper subject" of the novel. What fits her to be the heroine of a work so international in its terms of treatment is the special quality of her innocence, which is as American as that of Isabel Archer herself, and as different as possible from the blankness of the European *jeune fille*. It is the Prince who makes this clear in the midst of his reflection about the waters on which he floats: "What was it but history, . . . to have the assurance of the enjoyment of more money than [his ancestor] the palace-builder himself could have dreamed of? This was the element that bore him up and into which Maggie scattered, on occasion, her exquisite colouring drops. They were of the colour—of what on earth? of what but the extraordinary American good faith? They were of the colour of her innocence, and

yet at the same time of her imagination, with which their relation, his and these people's was all suffused" (I, 10). What he says aloud is, "You Americans are almost incredibly romantic" (I, 11). His sense of her difference from himself is revealed not only in the conversation with Fanny Assingham in which he defines in the extended image of the lightning elevator and the ruined old castle stairway the difference in the moral sense of Anglo-Saxons and Romans, and asks Fanny's help in understanding the Ververs, but also when he says to Charlotte, "it 's almost terrible, you know, the happiness of young good generous creatures. It rather frightens one. But the Blessed Virgin and all the Saints . . . have her in their keeping" (I, 52).

The enlightenment of the tragic and comic course of the action is to come to this particular kind of generous innocence, which James has regularly presented as characteristically American. He is using Fanny Assingham to announce the plan of the novel when he makes her say to her husband, "I never spoke [the truth] more, at all events, than when I declared . . . that Maggie was the creature in the world to whom a wrong thing could least be communicated. It was as if her imagination had been closed to it, her sense altogether sealed. That therefore . . . is what will now *have* to happen. Her sense will have to open" (I, 384). And so Maggie is launched on the tortuous and tortured way in which this last of James's pretty little American girls in Europe is to become one of his most calculating and controlled women. When the Prince takes her in his arms at the end of the novel, saying, "I see nothing but *you*" (II, 369), what he sees can surely no longer be "how extraordinarily *clear* . . . she had looked, in her prettiness" (I, 9), however much more wholly in love with her he is. She has won her husband by becoming more fully human; but this has meant to participate in the human traits of deception and cruelty, a cruelty which is made none the less actual by her pitying the victim of it. If comedy is given even the simple definition of a happy

ending, this is one of the most ambiguous of James's comedies, for Maggie has purchased "happiness" with her husband at the cost of her own separation from her father and his from her and of exile for Charlotte, who—as critics have often pointed out—is made to bear all the punish-ment for a crime to which Amerigo has been at least a party.

In achieving her end, Maggie grows from the inno-cent whom the other characters have at first thought of shielding from the knowledge of evil into the conscious manipulator of the destinies of the two couples. She suc-ceeds by learning to play a complicated game and conceal her hand. She acts her part in the comedy she arranges and never betrays the anguish her performance costs. She is herself transformed in the process; but the steps of her development are wholly convincing. James does not let her enlightenment begin until he has shown her as blind to the point of stupidity in her absorption in her father, with the consequent throwing together of Charlotte and Amerigo. Her invasion of the Verver household with the Principino and all the child's attendants and paraphernalia is comically treated in Charlotte's description of it to Amerigo. But the very fact of James's letting the ludicrous picture come from Charlotte is a reminder of what her own reaction is bound to be. The domesticity established by Maggie and her father makes the others bear all the re-sponsibility of representing the family in Society; but Maggie has no sense of the anomaly of this arrangement. It is only the lovers' protracting their stay at Matcham and going from there to Gloucester which finally begins to make her open her eyes. The first step which she takes is modest enough not to seem incongruous with her earlier simplicity. She merely decides to surprise Amerigo by decking herself out in unaccustomed finery and receiving him at home instead of awaiting him in Eaton Square. "These were small variations and mild manoeuvres, but they went accompanied on Maggie's part . . . with an in-

finite sense of intention" (II, 9). The long reflection surrounding this episode which begins Part II of the novel and
turns from the Prince to Maggie as center of consciousness
is a masterly foreshortening of her growing awareness of
"moving for the first time in her life as in the darkening
shadow of a false position" (II, 6). The presentation from
her own viewpoint of the intensity of her desire to preserve her marriage without breaking any of the terms of
her life, or acknowledging that they have been marred,
helps to make plausible the rapidity with which she develops. On the night of the return of the lovers from
Gloucester, her passion puts her in the power of her
husband's tenderness.

> She gave up, let her idea go, let everything go; her
> one consciousness was that he was taking her again
> into his arms. . . . Her acceptance of it, her response
> to it, inevitable, foredoomed, came back to her later
> on as a virtual assent to the assumption he had thus
> made that there was really nothing such a demon-
> stration did n't anticipate and did n't dispose of, . . .
> He had been right, overwhelmingly right, as to the
> felicity of his tenderness and the degree of her sensi-
> bility, but even while she felt these things sweep
> all others away she tasted of a sort of terror of the
> weakness they produced in her (II, 28-29).

And so she begins to play the complicated game of appearances and constructs the comedy which is to make her
tragic awareness. She becomes actress and director as well;
and the others play out their parts at her bidding. But
she organizes the desperate comedy at the cost of tragic
suffering. It is her reflection that she has "something to
do" and that she "must n't be weak for this" (II, 29) which
explains her vigorous entering into Society in order to
shift the relations among the couples and her being so
soon able to resist Amerigo when he draws her toward
him in the carriage, resorting to his "unfailing magic" (II,
56). She has had much more practice in controlling her
feelings and acting her part by the time she confronts him

with the "real knowledge" (II, 201) which has come to her through the purchase of the flawed bowl; and the quietness with which she conducts the scene and makes clear her advantage shows how "deep" (II, 202) she has become. It is the scene in which by her own declaration she ceases to be as she was: ceases "*Not* to know" (II, 202). It is also the scene in which she realizes that it is her husband who is at sea while "she kept her feet" (II, 203).

But she wins her victory of love by helping him. "It had operated within her now to the last intensity, her glimpse of the precious truth that by her helping him, helping him to help himself, as it were, she should help him to help *her*. Had n't she fairly got into his labyrinth with him?—was n't she indeed in the very act of placing herself there for him at its centre and core, whence, on that definite orientation and by an instinct all her own, she might securely guide him out of it?" (II, 187). She achieves her end by the supreme self-control to which she has disciplined herself and by the wisdom her love has taught her of helping him to help her. As she thinks of making her care for her father's serenity "her paramount law" (II, 203), she is aware of how much her husband does help her. "More strangely even than anything else her husband seemed to speak now but to help her in this. 'I know nothing but what you tell me'" (II, 203). Amerigo behaves always as the Prince he is. But in the course of losing her American innocence, Maggie has brought him from being an Italian man of the world whose "notion of a recompense to women—similar in this to his notion of an appeal—was more or less to make love to them" (I, 21-22) to being a man deeply in love with her.

She begins to feel sure of his allegiance exactly as she knows him to be at sea; but neither her enlightenment nor her task is yet fully accomplished. She has to act harder than ever to deal with Charlotte, who is now left to grope alone. Maggie sees her under the image of a caged wild beast; and she thinks of herself as the "over-

worked little trapezist girl" (II, 302). Part of her acro-
batic artistry has been the repeated lie with which she has
assured Charlotte that she has not felt wronged in answer
to Charlotte's questioning her in the intensely dramatic
scene on the terrace at Fawns, which ends with the "high
publicity" of the "prodigious kiss" exchanged by the antagonists (II, 252, 251). Her sense of crisis at Charlotte's
approach is conveyed by the violent image of her feeling
that she has "been thrown over on her back with her neck
from the first half-broken and her helpless face staring up"
(II, 242). The extravagance of her images throughout her
reflections has been one of the ways in which James has
revealed her as romantic; and her continuing to feel in
terms of such mental pictures while she is learning to look
at reality is part of what makes her development convincing. But this most extreme of her images also sharpens
awareness of her being in extremity—not just of fear of
Charlotte as her adversary but also of the weapons she
now finds herself about to use. Part of her dread of the
confrontation is shrinking from this further enlightenment
about herself.

The mixed effect of the whole last half of the novel
is due in large part to the mixed reaction to Maggie's
behavior. The complexity of her own feelings is demonstrated especially in the long conversation with her father
in the garden at Fawns, which parallels the one in Part I
in which she makes him realize that he must marry. The
realization which comes to him this time is that his marriage now requires his departing with his wife. The re-
minders of the earlier scene emphasize the extent of Maggie's development. Mr. Verver's images of "nun" and
"nymph" (I, 188) were then appropriate enough to Maggie,
however comically inconsistent with each other. Her
selfishness in the first conversation has been totally unconscious. Here, she insists on the fact of it in a way which
suggests that the self-accusation is something of a relief;
and her candor about the "most abysmal and unutterable

way of all" (II, 262) in which she loves Amerigo wins sympathy for her when she adduces him as the cause of her selfishness. Yet what she says of herself is true: she is willing to sacrifice her father, who chooses to help her, as well as Charlotte, whom she sees as dragged away to her doom by the "long silken halter looped round her beautiful neck" (II, 287). Her pity for Charlotte and her giving her rival the triumph of thinking Maggie stupid keep Maggie from being obnoxious in her own triumph; but they do not conceal her willingness to achieve her end at the price of suffering. Beyond all questions of judging her, even of liking or disliking her, James creates the feeling in these final scenes of her being intensely human in her own mixed feelings and in her having learned to reckon with the real world of fallible humanity, in which neither she nor her happiness can be wholly without corruption. The end is not, like that of *The Reverberator,* a restoring of comic balance after threatened tragedy. It is a comic balance which includes tragedy and keeps in uneasy equilibrium with the final embrace the echo of the Prince's words, "Everything's terrible, cara—in the heart of man" (II, 349).

IV ~ Comedy As Satiric Definition of Evil

Fools Who Cause Tragic Suffering

Throughout James's fiction there is a host of minor characters whose comic presentation increases awareness of tragedy. They give the feeling of a richly peopled world and by their actual multiplicity suggest a limitless range of possible ironies. James incisively outlines even such insignificant characters as Mrs. Tarrant and Mrs. Condrip; and the multitude of clearly pictured figures in the background not only gives the effect of a thickly inhabited world in which the main characters move, but also extends the pervasive sense of comedy and tragedy as inextricably linked. The central ironies gain resonance from the reverberations in this world of ironies.

Perhaps the largest group of minor characters in James's fictional world is that of the fools who are "the fixed constituents of almost any reproducible action." They are treated with derision and are allowed interest only as

they "minister, at a particular crisis, to the intensity of the free spirit engaged with them. The fools are interesting by contrast, by the salience they acquire, and by a hundred other of their advantages; and the free spirit, always much tormented, and by no means always triumphant, is heroic, ironic, pathetic or whatever, and, as exemplified in the record of Fleda Vetch, for instance, 'successful,' only through having remained free" (*The Art of the Novel*, pp. 129-30). James's treatment of the fools who make Fleda suffer in *The Spoils of Poynton* is a good example of his use of comedy to present the "fatal fools" and the way in which "the troubled life mostly at the centre of our subject—whatever our subject, for the artistic hour, happens to be—embraces them and deals with them for its amusement and its anguish: they are apt largely indeed, on a near view, to be all the cause of its trouble" (*The Art of the Novel*, p. 67).

The introduction of Mona Brigstock follows the impression of Waterbath, where the ugliness is "fundamental and systematic, the result of the abnormal nature of the Brigstocks, from whose composition the principle of taste had been extravagantly omitted" (*The Spoils of Poynton*, etc., p. 6). James uses the units in the description of the seat of the Brigstocks to forecast not only Mona's total absence of taste, but the particulars of her make-up. Just as the house is smothered "with trumpery ornament and scrapbook art" (p. 7), Mona is "strangely festooned" (p. 9). In the house, "the worst horror was the acres of varnish, something advertised and smelly, with which it was smeared: it was Fleda Vetch's conviction that the application of it, by their own hands and hilariously shoving each other, was the amusement of the Brigstocks on rainy days" (p. 7). Similarly, Mona is shown in the midst of the beauty of the Poynton gardens admiring instead "the sheen of her patent-leather shoes, which resembled a man's" (p. 28), and she first enters "making a familiar joke of" the walk to church, "scrambling" up the bank "laughing and

even romping" (p. 9). This connection with the deliberate bad taste and thoughtless high spirits of her family projects Mona as a figure of extravagant farce; but the suffering which the hideousness of Waterbath has already caused Mrs. Gereth and Fleda gives an abrasive underside to the picture of the tasteless hoyden who tumbles into the scene with Owen dangling beside her. Her actual entrance is the fulfillment of Mrs. Gereth's nightmare image when she has asked "herself with a terrible chill if fate could really be plotting to saddle her with a daughter-in-law brought up in such a place" (p. 8).

It is not, however, Mona's animal spirits and her absence of taste which chiefly give her the power to do harm. James endows her with a force of will as strong and unyielding as Mrs. Gereth's own; and the battle is joined between the two stubborn combatants the moment they encounter each other. It is the contest between these two inflexible women, so different in their kinds of blindness, which largely creates the suffering of Fleda, who sees. Mrs. Gereth's speaking of "Mona's hatred" comes as a surprise to Fleda; but "she certainly had not needed Mrs. Gereth to tell her that in close quarters that young lady would prove secretly mulish" (p. 18). James promptly shows the girl being quite openly "mulish" on her visit to Poynton, where Owen brings her to see if she approves what he has to offer her. In the presence of Mrs. Gereth's treasures and the harmonious work of art created by the whole of Poynton, she sits like a "bored tourist" exercising with "large levity" the "responsibility of observation. . . . Mona was not so stupid as not to see that something, though she scarcely knew what, was expected of her that she could n't give; and the only mode her intelligence suggested of meeting the expectation was to plant her big feet and pull another way" (pp. 25-26). Her only displays of animation are when she tells Fleda how she would improve the place by throwing out a winter garden and when she adroitly catches from her seat in the carriage the lady's magazine,

the "horrible thing with patterns for antimacassars" (p. 27), which Mrs. Brigstock has offered to leave for the improvement of Poynton. Mrs. Gereth after twenty-four hours of tortured politeness has tossed the periodical after her guests in a gesture of defiance which in its flamboyance suggests Becky Sharp's hurling of the famous Dictionary. But Mrs. Gereth is to have no such success in casting off all that her missile stands for. Mona's big feet remain planted until Mrs. Gereth's own too clever contriving and Fleda's oversubtle sense of fair play give Mona both Owen and the spoils of Poynton.

～　　　～　　　～

Fleda's suffering at the ugliness of the struggle over the treasures is complicated by her acute embarrassment at the way in which Mrs. Gereth champions her as their only possible guardian and therefore as the only possible wife for Owen. James's treatment insists on the sordidness of the squabble and Fleda's consequent distress. Mrs. Gereth absconds with the spoils "by as brilliant a stroke as any commemorated in the annals of punished crime" (p. 75), one which in Fleda's agonized recognition "belonged to the class of operations essentially involving the protection of darkness" (p. 74), and which the Brigstocks say is "simply stealing" (p. 97). It is the pivotal irony of the novel that having guessed from Mrs. Brigstock the carefully guarded secret of Owen's passion for Fleda, Mrs. Gereth restores the spoils in another adroit maneuver to achieve her end of making Fleda their custodian. What she actually achieves, of course, is making inevitable Owen's marriage with Mona, who will now never be the one to break off the engagement, as Fleda has said she must do before Fleda herself can become engaged to Owen. Fleda's loss of the chance of happiness is thus brought about by a compli-

cated interplay of her own scrupulousness[1] with the un-
scrupulousness of Mona and Mrs. Gereth.

On the surface Mrs. Gereth's fate looks like straightforward punishment neatly growing out of the crime committed. But James has taken pains to show that she is far
from being a simple villain; and his handling of her
throughout with a subtle mixture of mockery for her obsession and sympathy for her suffering has made her a
much more complex and much more interesting kind of
fool than Mona, who has no complicating virtues and is
held up to unrelieved ridicule. Though James declares in
the Preface that "she was not intelligent, was only clever"
(*The Art of the Novel*, p. 131), and her intelligence is not
his high lucidity, he endows her with marked powers. Her
strength of mind and her passion make her a much more
serious threat to Fleda exactly because she believes in her
own "deep morality" (p. 73) and wants to use the girl to
serve an end more important to her than any personal feeling. Fleda saw "how little vulgar avidity had to do with
this rigour. It was not the crude love of possession; it was
the need to be faithful to a trust and loyal to an idea"
(p. 46). But her obsession with an idea makes her all the
more ruthless in sacrificing human beings. Her insensi-
tiveness in choosing the time when Fleda and Owen have
both come early to breakfast as the moment to propose
her protégée as the proper mistress of Poynton is matched
only by her sincere bewilderment at the girl's pain and
indignation. Fleda's later protest involves explaining to
the older woman what there is to protest about. She finally
wins some acknowledgment; but she feels that it comes
simply as a concession in order to placate her rather than
from any understanding of the shame she has felt at being

1. For diametrically opposite judgments of Fleda's scruples, see the
treatments of the novel in Sister M. Corona Sharp, O.S.U., *The
Confidante in Henry James: Evolution and Moral Value of a Fictive
Character* (University of Notre Dame, 1963), especially pp. 114, 115;
and Laurence Bedwell Holland, *The Expense of Vision: Essays on
the Craft of Henry James* (Princeton, 1964), especially pp. 106, 112.

openly thrown at Owen: "it struck the girl that the admission was only made to please her and that Mrs. Gereth was secretly surprised at her not being as happy to be sacrificed to the supremacy of a high standard as she was happy to sacrifice her. She had taken a tremendous fancy to her, but that was on account of the fancy—to Poynton of course —taken by Fleda herself" (p. 37). The truth that Fleda discovers from the experience is "simply that all Mrs. Gereth's scruples were on one side and that her ruling passion had in a manner despoiled her of her humanity" (p. 37). James frequently holds her up to a mockery as spirited as that which he applies to Mona. There is lightness in the irony of most of the early comments on her obsession. "She had an idea, for it was her ambition, that she successfully made a secret of that awkward oddity her proneness to be rendered unhappy by the presence of the dreadful. Her passion for the exquisite was the cause of this, but it was a passion she considered she never advertised nor gloried in" (p. 6). Similarly, the comment when she suffers from the taste in her brother-in-law's house in Cadogan Place is: "The great drawback of Mrs. Gereth's situation was that, thanks to the rare perfection of Poynton, she was condemned to wince wherever she turned" (p. 12). But into the light mockery James insistently inserts the idea of derangement. This idea occurs to Fleda as she listens to the account of the treasures of Poynton. "They were present to Mrs. Gereth, her companion could see, with a vividness that at moments almost ceased to be that of sanity" (p. 15). As she prepares for the visit of the Brigstocks at Poynton, "Mrs. Gereth, even as she whisked away linen shrouds, persuaded herself of the likelihood on Mona's part of some bewildered blankness, some collapse of admiration that would prove disconcerting to her swain —a hope of which Fleda at least could see the absurdity and which gave the measure of the poor lady's strange, almost maniacal disposition to thrust in everywhere the question of 'things,' to read all behaviour in the light of

some fancied relation to them" (p. 24). This feeling of near dementia is the undercurrent of the comedy of the breakfast table scene. Owen smiles at Fleda with an appeal for understanding; "Fleda, however, mainly understood that Mrs. Gereth, with an odd wild laugh, held her so hard as to hurt her" (p. 30). In the midst of her passionate proclaiming of the religion of the "things," she suddenly inflicts on Fleda "a kiss intended by every sign to knock her into position" (p. 31). James increases the hint of aberration by referring to Don Quixote. "Her handsome, high-nosed excited face might have been that of Don Quixote tilting at a windmill" (p. 31).

Her own feeling of high-mindedness and her commitment to a cause beyond herself create a kind of blind fanaticism more inimical to Fleda's free spirit even than Mona's stupid self-interest. Almost the first impression Fleda receives of her is that she is "one of those who impose, who interfuse themselves" (p. 10). And in the whole course of the novel she is committing what is for James the cardinal sin of trying to manipulate another human being. As Fleda heard her account of her interview with Mrs. Brigstock, she "had listened in unbearable pain and growing terror, as if her companion, stone by stone, were piling some fatal mass upon her breast. She had the sense of being buried alive, smothered in the mere expansion of another will" (p. 209), and later in the scene Mrs. Gereth "again, with ferocity, embraced her young friend" (p. 211). Somewhat later, during their period of waiting to hear the results of Mrs. Gereth's miscalculated move of restoring the spoils, Fleda summons courage to say to her friend, "You simplify far too much. You always did and you always will. The tangle of life is much more intricate than you 've ever, I think, felt it to be. You slash into it . . . with a great pair of shears; you nip at it as if you were one of the Fates!" (p. 224). It is her oversimplifications that precipitate her own punishment and Fleda's, and Owen's fate as Mona's husband.

James is relentless in satirizing and showing the evil consequences of such blind use of power as Mrs. Gereth makes. Nevertheless, he does not withhold pity from her. Though "her ruling passion had in a manner despoiled her of her humanity" (p. 37), she still has the human power to suffer. Her anxiety over the things and her anguish over their loss are in exact proportion to her passionate commitment to their service. James presents wholly humorously, though not unsympathetically, Mrs. Gereth's suffering in the presence of ugliness; but the way "the poor lady's troubled soul ached" over her "inevitable surrender" (p. 15) of Poynton, he treats more seriously. As the threat to the "things" increases, he conveys the full intensity of her suffering. And finally, even though it is through her own folly that she has lost the chance to have Fleda as caretaker, she compels pity. "At last Mrs. Gereth too sank down again. Mrs. Gereth soundlessly wearily wept" (p. 244).

In juxtaposing Mona and Mrs. Gereth, James brings together in conflict two large classes of fools who are the "trouble" for the "free spirit engaged with them" throughout the course of his fiction. He depicts with incisive comedy a great many fools as wholly unsympathetic as Mona; and they range in folly from the brainlessness of Mrs. Weeks Wimbush in "The Death of the Lion," who virtually kills Neil Paraday with the stupid lionizing of the writer at Prestidge, to the astuteness of Mrs. Lowder in *The Wings of the Dove*, that "Britannia of the Market Place" who, if not directly implicated in the death of the heroine, represents the power which operates against Milly. She sits "in the midst of her money, founded on it and surrounded by it" (*The Wings of the Dove*, I, 30, 196), in the ostentatiously vulgar magnificence of the house at Lancaster Gate, as the symbol of the evil to be combated by the free spirits of the novel. James regularly uses unmitigatedly scornful laughter as the means of showing such fools for what they are: sources of the evil which

brings about tragic suffering. Just as regularly, he uses a more complicated presentation for more complicated fools who, like Mrs. Gereth, are clever but not "intelligent." Julia Dallow and Olive Chancellor, for instance, who try to control the lives of others in *The Tragic Muse* and *The Bostonians,* are full of misguided and harmful high-mindedness.

~   ~   ~

In addition to the fools who cause suffering to free spirits, there are a number—especially in the shorter fiction—who bring to grief more limited sympathetic characters. The satire of the destructive fools in such stories is heightened by the contrasting affectionate laughter at the foibles of the characters they destroy. One kind of limitation for which James regularly makes generous allowances is the unbridled romantic imagination that feeds itself on preposterously exalted notions of high life. He clearly enjoys Mrs. Rooth in *The Tragic Muse,* who moves "altogether in a world of elegant fable and fancy" and when she has nothing to eat begins "a novel in ten volumes" (*The Tragic Muse,* I, 219, 199). To Susan Stringham in *The Wings of the Dove* he gives perception and courage of an altogether higher order than Mrs. Rooth's, but he is throughout tenderly amused at her power to romanticize even in the depths of her intensely real suffering. One of his most indulgent treatments of romancing ladies is that of Mrs. Stormer in "Greville Fane," who can "invent stories by the yard, but [cannot] write a page of English" (*The Author of Beltraffio,* etc., p. 113). Unlike Mrs. Rooth, who escapes her poverty by reading sentimental novels, Mrs. Stormer in her heyday manages to avoid poverty by writing, under the pseudonym of Greville Fane, novels which make the staple of just such lending libraries as Mrs. Rooth frequents. "It would have been droll if it had n't been so

exemplary to see her tracing the loves of the duchesses beside the innocent cribs of her children" (pp. 121-22).
James intensifies both her emptiness of any sense of what
constitutes literature and her devotion to it as a profession
by making the narrator a writer who likes this "dull kind
woman" because she rests him "so from literature" (p. 113).
"She lived at ease . . . in those days—ease is exactly the
word, though she produced three novels a year. She scorned
me when I spoke of difficulty—it was the only thing that
made her angry" (p. 115).

The choice of a writer who does feel "the torment
of form" to tell the story also gives James freedom to use
the narrator's disgust in depicting the selfish rapacity of
the son and daughter who literally work their mother to
death to provide them with luxuries after the market for
her works is gone. The teller of the tale says of his confrontation with the son Leolin on the night of his mother's
death, "To meet him, to greet him, I had to make a sharp
effort; for the air he wore to me as he stood before me was
quite that of his mother's murderer" (p. 111). Mrs. Stormer,
since she regards a novelist's life as a "comfortable support,"
has brought Leolin up "to follow it" (p. 117). She does
this by giving him experience, which "was another name
for spoiling him with the best conscience in the world" (p.
121). He has lived a life of luxury and dissipation while
his mother's life as novelist has been his "comfortable
support." "She held, not unjustly, that the sincere novelist should feel the whole flood of life; she acknowledged
with regret that she had n't had time to feel it herself, and
the lapse in her history was in a manner made up by the
sight of its rush through this magnificent young man" (p.
128). "She was weary and spent at last, but confided to me
that she could n't afford to pause. She continued to speak of
her son's work as the great hope of their future . . . though
the young man wore to my sense an air more and more
professional if you like, but less and less literary. There
was at the end of a couple of years something rare in the

impudence of his playing of his part in the comedy" (p. 127). He continues to hoodwink his mother, who dies under the fond illusion that he never writes a line because he is so fastidious. She employs him to bring home material, the substance to which she will give form. "That was now his employ—he foraged for her in the great world at a salary" (p. 133).

The daughter, who despises Leolin, works with him only "to keep their mother at her desk" (p. 124). She is openly scornful of her mother, whom she berates for letting the prices of her work go down. She has fought her way into society by sheer rudeness and has finally achieved marriage with Sir Baldwin Luard, "an irredeemable mediocrity" (p. 119). Mrs. Stormer is immensely proud of this acquisition of a title and writes three novels to pay for a splendid wedding. It is Lady Luard's subsequent refusal to let her mother live with her, though "she suffered the inky fingers to press an occasional banknote into her palm" (p. 119), that finally breaks the brave spirit of the old lady. When the narrator goes to visit her in her cheap quarters, he finds her "wasted and wan" (p. 130). At last she begins to cry as she tells him of her rejection by her daughter and by her public alike. "I had never seen her break down and I was proportionately moved; she sobbed like a frightened child over the extinction of her vogue and the exhaustion of her vein" (p. 131). The narrator sees the suffering of Mrs. Stormer as pathetic rather than tragic; but he conveys all its pitiful reality. The comedy by which James defines the evil that causes the suffering is especially harsh in its satiric tone because it is narrated by a partisan of the sufferer.

The satire of the selfish children in "Greville Fane" is matched by that of the selfish mother in "Europe." Again James uses as narrator an observer whose sympathies are aroused by the plight of the victims, the three daughters of the prodigiously old Mrs. Rimmle, who themselves grow to extreme old age while she frustrates their dreams

of going to Europe by having a seizure whenever their departure is imminent. She is the "widow of a great public
character—as public characters were understood at Brook-
bridge . . . [who] was understood to have made, in his
wife's company, the tour of Europe at a date not immensely removed from that of the Battle of Waterloo" (*The
Author of Beltraffio*, etc., p. 342). The idea of a return
visit has first come up years before the story opens as the
suggestion that "she should go to Europe with her daughters and for her health. Her health was supposed to require constant support; but when it had at that period
tried conclusions with the idea of Europe it was not the
idea of Europe that had been insidious enough to prevail"
(p. 343). The daughters have, nevertheless, been brought
up with the vision of going to Europe. "They were all
growing old in the yearning to go, but Jane's yearning was
the sharpest" (p. 345). She and Becky, who "as the most
literary, had most mastered the subject" (p. 343), are within
three days of departure when the narrator is taken by his
sister-in-law to make his first call on them:

> "I positively desire, I really quite insist that
> they shall go," the old lady explained to us from
> her stiff chair. We 've talked about it so often, and
> they 've had from me so clear an account—I 've
> amused them again and again with it—of what's to
> be seen and enjoyed. If they 've had hitherto too
> many duties to leave, the time seems to have come
> to recognise that there are also many duties to *seek*.
> Wherever we go we find them—I always remind the
> girls of that. There's a duty that calls them to those
> wonderful countries, just as it called, at the right
> time, their father and myself—if it be only that of
> laying-up for the years to come the same store of
> remarkable impressions, the same wealth of knowl-
> edge and food for conversation as, since my return,
> I 've found myself so happy to possess." Mrs.
> Rimmle spoke of her return as of something of the
> year before last, but the future of her daughters
> was somehow, by a different law, to be on the scale
> of great vistas, of endless aftertastes. I think that,

without my being quite ready to say it, even this
first impression of her was somewhat upsetting; there
was a large placid perversity, a grim secrecy of intention, in her estimate of the ages (pp. 345-46).

Of course she does not allow the trip to take place. As
James puts it in the Preface, she "announced her approaching end—only to postpone it again after the plan was
dished and the flight relinquished" (*The Art of the Novel,*
p. 239).

When Jane finally does leave in spite of one of her
mother's seizures and refuses to come home, the old
woman speaks of her as dead. "Magnificent Becky" (p.
360) finances Jane in Europe while she herself is gradually
worn to death by her care of old Mrs. Rimmle. "She had
been ill for years, but the other state of health in the con-
templation of which she had spent so much of her life
had left her till too late no margin for heeding it" (p. 367).
So poor Maria is left alone to care for "the centenarian
mummy in the high chair" (p. 368) and to utter a bleak
"Never" to the narrator's suggestion that she will eventually
join Jane in Europe (p. 368). The story closes with Mrs.
Rimmle summoning the force, after preliminary gasps,
to speak:

"Have you heard where Becky's gone?" the wonderful witch's white lips then extraordinarily asked.

It drew from Maria, as on my previous visit, an
uncontrollable groan, and this in turn made me take
time to consider. As I considered, however, I had an inspiration. "To Europe?"

I must have adorned it with a strange grimace, but
my inspiration had been right. "To Europe," said Mrs.
Rimmle (p. 369). To this small drama, James himself in
the Preface applies the word tragedy: "Striking to the last
degree, I thought, that obscure, or at least that muffled,
tragedy" (*The Art of the Novel,* p. 239). Part of what
makes the tragedy of the daughters striking is the dreadful
comedy of Mrs. Rimmle.

From the cousin and his so-called "Countess" in "Four Meetings" to Abel Gaw in *The Ivory Tower* James depicts such selfish fools with a satire so severe as barely to stay within the confines of comedy. But he is realist enough to leave them usually having the last word, as Mrs. Rimmle does, whether or not their victims belong to the company of free spirits.

~ ~ ~

There is still another trouble-making kind of fool whom James finds of perennial interest. In a notebook entry concerning a proposal from Henry Harper that he write a "little international story on American snobbishness abroad," he writes: "But the only way that's at all luminous to look at it is to see what there may be in it of most eloquent, most illustrative and most human—most characteristic and essential: what is its real, innermost, dramatic, tragic, comic, pathetic, ironic *note*" (*Notebooks*, p. 176). The "note" which is such a mixture James often strikes in depicting characters who, without being clever like Mrs. Gereth, cause trouble and themselves draw mixed response. *The Tragic Muse* can be said to end happily, though Nick's artistic life seems jeopardized by his agreeing to paint Julia's portrait. But the whole novel has as mixed a note as the one James describes, and he does not let any of its fools appear as villains. One of the most amusing of the fools is Lady Agnes, Nick's mother and certainly one of the causes of his "trouble" as he tries to give up politics and become a serious artist, since she thinks that "art's pardonable only so long as it's bad" (*The Tragic Muse*, I, 18). At first she seems merely a ludicrous caricature of a stage dowager when she admonishes her daughter, "Don't be vulgar, Grace" and then repeats to Biddy "Don't be vulgar" (I, 11, 12); or when she gets up "to signify that enough had been said about people and

questions she had never so much as heard of" (I, 68). But
the laughter becomes mixed as it is directed toward her
effort to control her natural domineeringness. There is
pathos in her struggles to show tact in her effort to compel
Nick to fulfill the political career of her husband, whose
memory she idolizes. "Fortunately she was a woman of
innumerable discretions, and a part of the worn look that
sat in her face came from her having schooled herself for
years, in commerce with her husband and sons, not to
insist unduly. She would have liked to insist, nature had
formed her to insist, and the self-control had told in more
ways than one. Even now it was powerless to prevent her
suggesting that before doing anything else Nick should at
least repair to the inn and see if there were n't some tele-
grams" (I, 72). In the scenes in which she does insist, her
limitations are even more apparent; but her suffering in
her thwarted maternal ambition is pitiable. "You know
what Percival is and the comfort I have of him. You know
the property and what he 's doing with it and what comfort I get from *that!* Everything's dreary but what you can
do for us. Everything's odious, down to living in a hole
with one's girls who don't marry. Grace is impossible—
I don't know what's the matter with her; no one will look
at her, and she's so conceited with it—sometimes I feel as
if I could beat her! And Biddy will never marry, and
we 're three dismal women in a filthy house; and what are
three dismal women, more or less, in London?" (I, 250-51).
James often shows suffering as the result of imagination.
He says of Nick, for instance, that "He paid the heavy
price of the man of imagination" (II, 74). But in the
rendering of Lady Agnes's woe he shows how little a limited imagination is a guarantee against suffering. He
presents her as a figure wholly pathetic in her anguish
over what she regards as Nick's defection when he gives
up his seat in Parliament. She looked like a "woman who
had received her death-blow" (II, 226). But her very
suffering is blind and selfish, and her capacity to feel pain

makes her all the more an obstacle to Nick's free spirit. It is, in fact, her power to suffer that makes her a real problem for him: "he had been ready to disappoint his mother—he had not been ready to destroy her" (II, 181). James shows her as undestroyed and laughable to the end; but the comedy is enriched by pathos. The element of pathos, instead of weakening the impression of the power of such fools, makes them seem all the more humanly the cause of all the trouble.

V ~ Partly Tragic Minor Characters

Characters like Lady Agnes, while they evoke a response that includes pity, are still used to make clear what the free spirits must combat. There are many other characters both comic and pathetic in themselves who are not arrayed against the heroes and are frequently their companions. These characters are not part of the satiric definition of evil, but simply part of what James saw as reality, which is both comic and tragic.

Tragedy is latent in even so minor a comic figure as Mark Ambient's medieval looking sister in "The Author of Beltraffio" who, her brother thinks, makes "up very well as a Rossetti" (*The Author of Beltraffio*, etc., p. 25). She always has the air of bearing evil tidings and her manner is "habitually that of such a prophetess of ill" (p. 70) that the narrator hesitates to believe her when she speaks with "horrible insistence" of the murder (p. 71). Her poses are ridiculous; and she belongs as much as Bunthorne does to the satire of the aestheticism of the late nineteenth century. But she is not part of the evil which creates the

tragedy in the story and James shows her pitiableness as a "restless romantic disappointed spinster" (p. 24).

Lady Aurora in *The Princess Casamassima* is a much more endearingly comic and pathetic old maid. She is revealed on her first appearance as a person of much finer grain than Miss Ambient; but she is certainly partly ridiculed in the opening description: "Her clothes looked as if she had worn them a good deal in the rain, and the note of a certain disrepair in her apparel was given by a hole in one of her black gloves, through which a white finger gleamed" (*The Princess Casamassima,* I, 127). Yet when this "poor devoted, grotesque lady" (I, 136) speaks of herself as mad, laughter is obliterated by pity and admiration:

> I have my liberty, and that's the greatest blessing in life except the reputation of being queer, and even a little mad, which is a greater advantage still. I'm a little mad, you know; you need n't be surprised if you hear it. That's because I stop in town when they go into the country; all the autumn, all the winter, when there's no one here (except three or four millions) and the rain drips, drips, drips from the trees in the big dull park where my people live. I dare say I ought n't to say such things to you, but, as I tell you, I'm quite a proper lunatic and I might as well keep up the character. When one's one of eight daughters and there's very little money (for any of *us* at least) and nothing to do but go out with three or four others in mackintoshes, one can easily go off one's head (I, 251).

Slightly mad she may be, but she is the most admirable of the characters who surround the selfishly arrogant Muniments; and she is wholly pathetic in her hopeless passion for Paul. She is carefully fitted into the social texture of the novel; but it is clearly as part of the "aggregation of human life [of which London is] the most complete compendium in the world" (*Notebooks,* p. 28), that James finds her amusing and touching.

He often shows a similar mixture of the comic and

the pathetic in minor characters who are much closer to
his protagonists. Susan Stringham in *The Wings of the
Dove* is as laughable—and as endearing—as is Lady Aurora.
She has written romantic stories for the best magazines;
and she worships Guy de Maupassant. But when she
encounters Milly, she finds herself "in presence of the
real thing, the romantic life itself" (*The Wings of the
Dove*, I, 107). "This was poetry—it was also history—Mrs.
Stringham thought, to a finer tune even than Maeterlinck
and Pater, than Marbot and Gregorovius" (I, 111). It is
she who sees Milly as "one of the finest, one of the rarest
. . . cases of American intensity" (I, 116) and "the potential
heiress of all the ages" (I, 109); and it is she who throughout the novel insists on regarding the girl as a princess.
James gives Mrs. Stringham's "infinitely fine vibration"
(I, 105) to the young visitor from New York before he
gives any direct impression of Milly and thus colors the
reader's response in advance. To convey the feeling of
Milly's specialness James uses the prim Bostonian who,
wearing her pince-nez glasses, "opened, each evening, her
Transcript with the same interfusion of suspense and resig-
nation . . . [and] attended her almost daily concert with
the same expenditure of patience and the same economy
of passion" (I, 108). The comic presentation of Susan
helps to give reality to Milly, for Mrs. Stringham's feeling
at once raises the girl above ordinary humanity and keeps
her human. The exaltation of the heroine is authentic
and gives the dimension of greatness to her suffering. But
a direct presentation of it would have seemed merely
fatuous. James keeps his own adoration of Milly from
being oversolemn by letting it come through Mrs. Stringham, whose solemnities he can undercut by humor. The
extravagance of her attitude toward Milly is shown as
comical in itself; but the single-minded sincerity of her
devotion also mocks the mixed motives in the emulation
of it by Mrs. Lowder and Kate. When she renews connections with Mrs. Lowder, she knows that "whatever Mrs.

Lowder might have to show . . . she would have nothing like Milly Theale, who constituted the trophy producible by poor Susan" (I, 141). As for Kate, Susan thinks that "all the Kate Croys in Christendom were but dust for the feet of her Milly" (II, 45).

James makes Kate's finding Mrs. Stringham a bore and Mrs. Lowder's patronizing her as Milly's "funny friend" (I, 263) show up their own natures; and their condescension toward her forms a comic counterpart to their separate designs on Milly. Milly's resentment of Kate's attitude toward Susan shows that she is not superhumanly forgiving and provides for her some insight into Kate's character. She is too free of self-importance to understand that it is on Milly's own account that Susan has been taken up by Mrs. Lowder, whom she ought simply to have bored.

> Susan Shepherd at least bored the niece—that was plain; this young woman saw nothing in her—nothing to account for anything, not even for Milly's own indulgence: which little fact became in turn to the latter's mind a fact of significance. It was a light on the handsome girl—representing more than merely showed—that poor Susie was simply as nought to her. This was in a manner too a general admonition to poor Susie's companion, who seemed to see marked by it the direction in which she had best most look out. It just faintly rankled in her that a person who was good enough and to spare for Milly Theale should n't be good enough for another girl . . . yet in the end, be it added, she grasped the reason, and the reason enriched her mind. Was n't it sufficiently the reason that the handsome girl was, with twenty other splendid qualities, the least bit brutal too, and did n't she suggest, as no one yet had ever done for her new friend, that there might be a wild beauty in that, and even a strange grace? (I, 181-82).

James holds Susan firmly in a comic perspective. It is as ludicrous for her to see herself as the representative

of culture (I, 109) as for her to think that because she
has been sent to school at Vevey, she is a woman of the
world (I, 119). Her appearance always enhances the impression of the comical earnestness of the "pilgrim from
Boston" whether she is wearing her " 'handsome' felt hat,
so Tyrolese, yet somehow, though feathered from the eagle's
wing, so truly domestic" as she goes "about her usual
Boston business with her usual Boston probity" (I, 108)
or glittering in Milly's fancy of her as a fairy godmother
(I, 145) or showing to Milly's actual eye "the further
denudation . . . of her little benevolent back" (I, 263).
Even when she comes to Densher's rooms with the desolate
news that Milly has "turned her face to the wall" (II, 270),
her bedraggled appearance in her wet waterproof seems
laughable until the comment that "her face, under her
veil, richly rosy with the driving wind, was—and the veil
too—as splashed as if the rain were her tears" (II, 269).

And James never laughs at her tears. Indeed they
are peculiarly moving throughout the novel because they
are all shed on Milly's account and because she struggles
so heroically to protect Milly from them. After her first
session with the great doctor, Sir Luke Strett, when she
and Milly look rather than speak about what his judgment
portends, she manages to say, " 'I'm not worrying, Milly.'
And poor Susie's face registered the sublimity of her lie"
(II, 102). But when she goes to Lancaster Gate, she has to
begin her account of herself by asking permission to cry.
"She cried and cried at first—she confined herself to that;
it was for the time the best statement of her business. Mrs.
Lowder moreover intelligently took it as such, though
knocking off a note or two more, as she said, while Susie
sat near her table. She could resist the contagion of tears"
(II, 108). The scorn in James's picture of the imperturb-
able Mrs. Lowder intensifies both the response to Susan's
present distress and awareness of the hostile forces at work
against the person in whom her life centers.

Indeed Milly is her life. She has accepted the pro-

posal of the trip to Europe because, since she had no personal life to lead, "she honestly believed that she was thus
supremely equipped for leading Milly's own" (I, 113). All
that she wants for herself is the joy of allowing Milly to
be more completely her princess. The degree of her power
not to interfere is demonstrated early in the novel when
she follows Milly on her walk on the Brünig and sees her
seated precariously on the rock which seems to be poised
simply in gulfs of air. She not only stifles her cry of terror
at the moment; she refrains from mentioning later that
she has seen the girl looking down upon the kingdoms of
the earth. "For she now saw that the great thing she had
brought away was precisely a conviction that the future
was n't to exist for her princess in the form of any sharp
or simple release from the human predicament. It would n't
be for her a question of a flying leap and thereby of a
quick escape. It would be a question of taking full in the
face the whole assault of life, to the general muster of
which indeed her face might have been directly presented
as she sat there on her rock. . . . The image that thus
remained with the elder lady kept the character of a
revelation" (I, 125). In terms of this revelation she lives
her own life to the end, trying to help Milly carry out Sir
Luke's injunction, and her own longing, to *live*. After
the interview between Susan and Sir Luke, Milly knew that
"Susie positively wanted to suffer for her" (II, 124); but
she also knew that Susie would respect her refusal to be
an invalid and would allow her to meet her trouble in
her own way. After she goes to Venice, she reflects on
Eugenio that: "He had taken his place already for her
among those who were to see her through, and meditation
ranked him, in the constant perspective, for the final function, side by side with poor Susie—whom she was now
pitying more than ever for having to be herself so sorry and
to say so little about it. Eugenio had the general tact of a
residuary legatee—which was a character that could be
definitely worn; whereas she could see Susie, in the event

of her death, in no character at all, Susie being insistently, exclusively concerned with her mere makeshift duration" (II, 134).

James performs the remarkable feat of making Susan Stringham convincing as a person whose own identity is enhanced by her completely giving herself up to leading another person's life. When she comes to Densher's rooms, he has the feeling that she is so "decidedly wonderful" that she can see in them all their connection with Kate. "He saw, and it stirred him, that she had n't come to judge him; had come rather, so far as she might dare, to pity. This showed him her own abasement—that, at any rate, of grief; and made him feel with a rush of friendliness that he liked to be with her" (II, 273). When he later thinks gratefully of the way she has protected both Milly and himself from Mrs. Lowder's curiosity: "she had suppressed explanations and connexions, and indeed, for all he knew, blessed Puritan soul, had invented commendable fictions" (II, 339), the terms of his reflection show the same glint of humor mingled with affection which has marked James's whole presentation of the comical and admirable and wholly human pilgrim from Boston.

~   ~   ~

Mrs. Stringham lives at a high level of perception, which springs from her romantic nature and from her adoration of Milly. But she is totally devoid of a sense of humor, and the absence of comic awareness is partly the reason that she herself is comic as well as appealing. In Madame Grandoni James portrays with equal success a realist, whose comic perception plays over all she observes —including herself. But what James calls the "drollery" of her mocking comments early shows the fundamental seriousness of her view of life; and the development of "her scent for disaster," which grows more and more "dismally

acute" (*The Princess Casamassima*, II, 274) contributes much to increasing apprehension in *The Princess Casamassima*.

James had presented her with obvious relish in *Roderick Hudson;* and he apparently felt of her, as he did of Christina, that she refused to be put away in the puppet box after that brief appearance. She presents herself in the later novel as "an honest, ugly, unfortunate German" (I, 210). While the bemused Hyacinth sits in Christina's theatre box, dazzled by the beauty and brilliance of the Princess, she is there "huddled together with her hands folded on her stomach and her lips protruding" as she follows the performance. "Several times, however, she turned her head to Hyacinth, and then her expression changed; she repeated the jovial, encouraging, almost motherly nod with which she had greeted him on his making his bow and by which she appeared to wish to intimate that, better than the serene beauty on the other side, she could enter into the full anomaly of his situation. She seemed to argue that he must keep his head and that if the worst should come to the worst she was there to look after him" (I, 209). The suggestion is more ominous than comforting. As she undercuts Christina's extravagance with her common sense and tries by her ridicule, both of the revolution and of the Princess's fanciful flights, to qualify Hyacinth's bewitchment, she is entirely cheerful. But James's presentation of this battered old woman who likes "people to bear their troubles as one has done one's self" (I, 283), as the only restraining influence on Christina, simply increases the feeling that the Princess will brook no restraint. As the old lady tells the Prince in her first talk with him, she is already aware that Christina may do things which will put staying with her out of the question. It becomes increasingly apparent that she will not be there when the worst comes to the worst, and that her presence would in any case be of no avail.

As in Mrs. Stringham's relation to Milly, part of Madame Grandoni's function is to interpret Christina by direct comment. Especially in the conversations with the Prince, James uses what she says to bring out the complexity of Christina's character. Her saying, "I've known her so long. And she has some such great qualities" (I, 272), is balanced by her acknowledgment of Christina's extravagance while thinking herself a model of thrift and by her refusing to promise the Prince not to leave his unpredictable wife: "Ah, let us not tangle ourselves up with promises! . . . You know the value of any engagement one may take with regard to the Princess; it's like promising you I'll stay in the bath when the hot water's on. When I begin to be scalded I've to jump out—naked as I may naturally be. I'll stay while I can, but I should n't stay if she were to do certain things. . . . I can't say what things. It's utterly impossible to predict on any occasion what Christina will do. She's capable of giving us great surprises. The things I mean are things I should recognise as soon as I saw them, and they would make me leave the house on the spot" (I, 275). Though she has met the Prince with her "florid, humorous face [elongated] to a degree that was almost comical" (I, 270), she has tried to bring him to some decent acceptance of the reality of his situation; and as she dismisses him, she cannot resist the fun of puzzling him: " 'It's the common people who please her,' she returned with her hands folded on her crumpled satin stomach and her ancient eyes, still keen for all comedy, raised to his face. 'It's the lower orders, the *basso popolo*' " (I, 278). But she underlines her feeling of Christina's instability when she comforts him: "Don't trouble yourself; it won't be for long!" (I, 278) upon which Hyacinth is perhaps too patly announced as a new caller. Madame Grandoni emphasizes the same theme at her next interview with the Prince, who is of course more troubled than ever after seeing Hyacinth. The young man, she assures him, is simply one of Christina's studies of the lower orders.

"She must try everything; at present she's trying democracy" (I, 305).

Madame Grandoni, with her sanity of observation, is as clear about Christina's integrity as about her capriciousness. She reminds the Prince that his great mistake in relation to his wife had been "treating a person (and such a person!) as if, as a matter of course, she lied. Christina has many faults, but she has n't that one; that's why I can live with her. She 'll speak the truth always" (I, 306). Even in the final interview with the Prince, when she realizes that she can no longer countenance by her presence the anarchistic activity which she senses though she refuses to observe it, she defends Christina against the Prince's frenziedly jealous accusations: "She *has* lovers—she *has* lovers" (II, 304). She finally makes him realize that Christina is not meeting Paul as his mistress: "She has gone to that house to break up society." But when this makes the Prince pronounce her "the Devil in person," the old woman, appalled as she too is by Christina's activities, is still perfectly clear about her good faith: "No, she 's not the Devil, because she wishes to do good" (II, 310). These conversations with the Prince exemplify the way James uses the clear-eyed old companion to guide interpretation of the contradictory character of his complicated heroine.

She serves also the dramatic function of marking in her own progression from a comic to a tragic view the movement of the novel toward disaster. The emphasis on her sanity and her early poise makes her increasing despair all the more portentous. Her loss of a sense of comedy is underlined by the visual impression of her increasing decrepitude. In the early scenes her look of age is simply part of the ludicrousness of her whole appearance and gives no impression of feebleness. But by the time of Hyacinth's visit to Medley, she has become anxious; and the impression of physical decline has begun. Her coming to warn him again recalls that her first warning has done no good so that the whole scene serves to enforce the feeling of his

doom. When Hyacinth on his ladder in the library stares down at her, he is struck with the "odd effect of Madame Grandoni's wig in that bird's-eye view" (II, 9). So far, there seems to be only mirth in the description; but as she shut the door in preparation for speaking more clearly and "advanced into the room again with her superannuated, shuffling step, walking as if her shoes were too big for her," the feeling of her physical feebleness colors what she says about wanting to be a friend to Hyacinth as well as to the Princess. Her "Perhaps it 's of no use" (II, 10), gives the feeling of the scene. Her own recognition of the probable futility of her urging Hyacinth to go home to-morrow comes out in her saying: "And sometimes I think I also shall go to-morrow!" (II, 11).

Of course Hyacinth does not go; and the old lady's anxiety has immeasurably increased by the time of Sholto's visit. Her exclamation, *"Santissima Vergine!* I 'm glad to see you" (II, 76), expresses only relief "There was nothing at present in the old lady's countenance of her usual spirit of cheer; it expressed anxiety and even a certain sternness, and the excellent woman had perhaps at this moment more than she had ever had in her life of the air of a duenna who took her duties seriously. She looked almost august. 'From the moment you come it's a little better. But it 's very bad. . . . Perhaps you 'll be able to tell me where Christina *veut en venir.* I 've always been faithful to her—I 've always been loyal. But to-day I 've lost patience. It has no sense' " (II, 77). She has told the Prince that she stays because she has thought she can do some good. Now she tells Sholto only that she does not leave because she fears to make the scandal worse.

After Christina has given up her great house and gone to live in mock poverty at Madeira Crescent, Madame Grandoni seems to have sunk into acceptance of "the situation too completely to fidget at such a trifle as her companion's not coming home at a ladylike hour" (II, 179). Later, on Christina's going out of the room, "Madame

Grandoni's eyes followed her and Hyacinth made out in them a considerable lassitude, a plaintive bewilderment and surrender" (II, 180-81). She groans as she wonders how it will all end "as some of Christina's economies were most expensive" (II, 184). What she fears most, however, is not the Prince's cutting off funds, but Christina's involvement in revolutionary connections which may end in her death. "The old lady wished to know how she would enjoy the hangman's rope" (II, 185). Hyacinth, far from being put off by her account of Christina, is more infatuated than ever; but he is not too lost in admiration to observe Madame Grandoni's depression: " 'I think that if I had been capable of quitting you I should have done it by this time: I 've neglected such opportunities,' the old woman sighed. Hyacinth now made out that her eye had quite lost or intermitted its fine old pleasantry: she was troubled about many things" (II, 187).

She has aged still more by her next appearance during Paul's visit. "Madame Grandoni appeared cautiously, creepingly, as if she did n't know what might be going on in the parlour" (II, 232). After Paul's departure, she taunts Christina with having paid her visit to Rosy in order to see Paul. "It was striking, the good humour with which the Princess received this rather coarse thrust, which could have been drawn from Madame Grandoni only by the petulance and weariness of increasing age and the antipathy she now felt to Madeira Crescent and everything it produced" (II, 233). The double effect of her physical and mental state is continued during the visit of Mr. Vetch. Earlier in the novel, she has been perfectly capable of "lifting her crumpled corpulence" (I, 308) out of her chair; but now Mr. Vetch has to help her to rise from the low armed chair in which "she had been immersed" (II, 234). Her parting words to him are, "You 're not a wicked revolutionary then? You 're not a conspirator nor an assassin? It surprises me, but so much the better. In this house one can never know. It 's not a good house, and if

you 're a respectable person it 's a pity you should come here. Yes, she 's very gay and I 'm very sad. I don't know how it will end. After me, I hope. The world's not good, certainly; but God alone can make it better. . . . I wander about. I 've no rest. . . . Good-night to you, whoever you are" (II, 239-40).

Before the final scene with the Prince, she is sitting motionless after her supper in "gloomy solitude" in the little back parlor. She is "staring at the crumpled cloth with her hands folded on the edge of the table" (II, 303) when she becomes aware of his presence; and she asks him for help in getting to the front room and the fire. The picture of his settling her with her shawl suggests extreme old age. She summons energy enough to give the Prince as just an account as she can of Christina, and to come to the final decision to leave. She is never more admirable than here where she faces, with the same realistic sense of honor which has always distinguished her, the fact that: "there 's nothing for me in decency at present but to pack my trunk. Judge by the way I 've tattled" (II, 315). On the appearance of Hyacinth, with his gift for opportune— or inopportune—entrances, the old lady departs. " 'My visitor 's going, but I 'm going too,' said Madame Grandoni. 'I must take myself to my room—I 'm falling to pieces. Therefore kindly excuse me' " (II, 316). James allows her after this "for an instant, as she tossed off a small satirical laugh, a return of her ancient drollery" (II, 317) when she warns the two men that if they talk long, Christina may come in. But the impression which remains is that of her real announcement that she has come to the end of her effort to ward off disaster: "I 'm falling to pieces."

Her departure, which James has steadily identified with the defeat of her hope of saving Christina, takes place; and all that is left to learn is the process of the final doom. When Hyacinth goes to Madeira Crescent for his last deso-lating visit to Christina, he does not know that Madame Grandoni has left; and on learning that Christina is out,

he asks for the old lady: "the desire was strong in him to
see once more, for the last time, the ancient afflicted titular
'companion' of the Princess, whom he had always liked.
She had struck him as ever in the slightly ridiculous position of a confidant of tragedy in whom the heroine, stricken
with reserves unfavourable to the dramatic progression,
should have ceased to confide" (II, 393). But for all her
being a confidante in whom the heroine has ceased to
confide, it is exactly to sharpen the effect of the dramatic
progression that James has most effectively used her. The
stages of her progress from comic to tragic spirit mark
the stages by which the novel moves to its catastrophe.

~ ~ ~

Maria Gostrey in *The Ambassadors* is a confidante
who retains the confidence of the hero. She is a realist and
a humorist as Madame Grandoni is; but there is nothing
grotesque in either her appearance or her manner. What
Strether notices when he first finds her facing him is her
"features—not freshly young, not markedly fine, but on
happy terms with each other" (*The Ambassadors*, I, 5). And
in spite of James's rather contrived way of introducing her
to Strether through her recognition of Waymarsh's name,
he manages to make her opening the conversation seem
consonant with Strether's attributing to her a "perfect
plain propriety," and finding her "thoroughly civilized"
(I, 8, 9).

Both in the Preface to *The Portrait of a Lady,* where
he links her with Henrietta Stackpole, and in the Preface
to *The Ambassadors,* James firmly relegates Maria to the
category of *ficelles;* but he acknowledges, with obvious
pleasure in what he has made of Maria, that if the *"ficelle*
character of the subordinate party" is artfully enough dis-
simulated, she may achieve "something of the dignity of a
prime idea" (*The Art of the Novel,* pp. 323, 324). From

the beginning of the novel James allows Maria the dignity
of a prime idea and thus makes more convincing her
functioning as *ficelle*. His way of doing this is to give her
personal tragedy to bear and to provide her with a sense
of comedy. He makes her a character who commands interest and sympathy as he launches her into the rôle of
ficelle. Strether's consciousness that she is leading him
forth into the world and showing him how to enjoy it
reveals quite as much of Maria's charm and good sense as
of Strether's responsiveness. In the whole play of her wit
and the friendly humor with which she laughs at herself
as "a general guide—to 'Europe'" (I, 18) while she is
initiating him into pleasures as diverse as walking on the
old town walls of Chester and ordering an English breakfast, James lets her present herself directly and makes
Strether's response to her believable. By the end of the
first book he has put her in the relation with Strether
which will enable her to fulfill her rôle as confidante and
has revealed in her the traits of eager curiosity and acute
perception which fit her for it. Part of what makes her so
excellent a *ficelle* is that she is so interesting a person in
herself; and James makes her the more interesting by showing under the light play of her "restless irony" (I, 44)
hints of something altogether more sober. The interchange
about her being an unpaid companion to her compatriots
in Europe has been gay enough; but when Strether asks,
"How do we reward you?" (I, 18) she hesitates and finally
answers, "You don't!" After a pause, she again directs
her "strange and cynical wit" (I, 19) toward Strether and
his fear of Waymarsh; but the hesitation surrounding her
answer as much as the response itself gives the moment a
special seriousness. It is perhaps too much to say that it
is portentous; but it comes back to mind when the last
sentence of the first book makes explicit Maria's feeling for
Strether. Thereafter it haunts the whole course of her
gallant service to him until his final ironic refusal to re-

ward her because of his feeling that he must get nothing for himself.

In London the "little confronted dinner," charms Strether with the intimacy of the "small table on which the lighted candles had rose-coloured shades" and at which Maria sits opposite him in a "cut down" dress and wearing "round her throat a broad red velvet band with an antique jewel . . . attached" (I, 50); and his response suggests at least the possibility of his falling in love with her, especially since his mental comparison of her with Mrs. Newsome presents an unconsciously satiric view of the lady of Woollett. But as James uses Strether's answers to Maria's questions to elucidate his situation, she is performing principally as *ficelle;* and part of this function is to serve Strether as interpreter. She sees more than he knows he is telling her about Chad, about Mrs. Newsome, and even about Sarah Pocock; and the particular quality of the humor of the scene, instinct as it is with tragical possibilities, comes largely from Maria's seeing further than Strether does. She tries gently to enlighten him about the woman who is keeping Chad in Paris:

> "Are you quite sure she 's very bad for him?"
> Something in his manner showed it as quite pulling him up. "Of course we are. Would n't *you* be?"
> "Oh I don't know. One never does—does one? —beforehand. One can only judge on the facts. Yours are quite new to me; I 'm really not in the least, as you see, in possession of them: so it will be awfully interesting to have them from you. If you 're satisfied, that's all that's required. I mean if you 're sure you *are* sure: sure it won't do."
> "That he should lead such a life? Rather!"
> "Oh but I don't know, you see, about his life; you 've not told me about his life. She may be charming—his life!"
> "Charming?"—Strether stared before him. "She 's base, venal—out of the streets."
> "I see" (I, 54-55).

Just as Strether misses the irony in her judgment of his view of Chad's entanglement, he is wholly unaware of the motive of her probing about Chad's mother, though her accurate description of Mrs. Newsome's hair does make him exclaim, "You 're the very deuce" (I, 67). She answers gaily, "What else *should* I be? It was as the very deuce I pounced on you. But don't let it trouble you, for everything but the very deuce—at our age—is a bore and a delusion, and even he himself, after all, but half a joy." This tone of self-mockery plays over all she says about herself in relation to Strether and is present in the mock heroics of her parting:

. . . "you shall succeed. And to that end I 'm yours—"

"Ah, dear lady!" he kindly breathed.

"Till death," said Maria Gostrey. "Good-night" (I, 75). But "that end" is success as Mrs. Newsome's ambassador because failure would make him lose "Everything." She has seen perfectly that he is not in love with Mrs. Newsome but that his future depends on her. The scene has admirably served the purpose of dramatic exposition; at the same time it has almost removed Maria's hope of winning Strether for herself.

The humorousness, as well as the devotion, with which she thereafter carries out her promise sustains awareness of her triumphant surmounting of selfishness and gives her increasingly the "dignity of a prime idea." Her having the personal significance of rising above her own tragedy to meet Strether's needs makes her steadily more interesting in her function as *ficelle*. Even her going off to Mentone because she cannot lie for Madame de Vionnet is a reminder of how much she herself cares for Strether. It is part of James's skill in manipulating her as *ficelle* to remove her from the scene while Strether falls completely under the spell of her exquisite rival; but it is the special mark of that skill that he makes humanly moving her inability to stay and help.

Though Strether has cried out in protest at her

abandoning him, he sees as clearly as she does after her
return that their relation has changed. He has learned, as
she puts it, "to toddle alone" (II, 48). He still reports to
her and marvels at her understanding and at how after an
interview with her, "he felt his sense of things cleared up
and settled" (II, 45). But he no longer depends on her in
the same way. There is irony beyond what he realizes in
his reflection that:

> . . . the time seemed already far off when he had
> held out his small thirsty cup to the spout of her
> pail. Her pail was scarce touched now, and other
> fountains had flowed for him; she fell into her place
> as but one of his tributaries; and there was a strange
> sweetness—a melancholy mildness that touched him
> —in her acceptance of the altered order.
>
> It marked for himself the flight of time, or at
> any rate what he was pleased to think of with irony
> and pity as the rush of experience; it had been but
> the day before yesterday that he sat at her feet and
> held on by her garment and was fed by her hand
> (II, 48-49).

During the period of the Pococks' visit, he comes to her
almost dutifully to report to her, feeling that it would
"amuse" her to hear of the doings of his world. "He was
sorry again, gratefully sorry she was so out of it—she who
had really put him in; but she had fortunately always her
appetite for news" (II, 132). She *is* amused and amusing
about the latest deputation from Woollett; understanding
as always, she gives Strether a chance to develop the implications of his dilemma and come only to the issue of saying,
"But there—as usual—we are!" (II, 142).

When he comes to see her at the end of the summer
to report that "they 're all off . . . at last" (II, 226), and
describes how Madame de Vionnet has captivated Jim
Pocock, Maria asks him point blank, "Are you really in
love with her?" (II, 228). He gives answer enough by
evading her question; and she speaks more frankly than
she has yet done of her "tremendous sense of privation"

(II, 229), which she explains as the feeling that she has ceased to serve him. When he assures her, "I want you here," the scene is restored to something of their usual tone of comic irony, "there you are" echoing through it as a sort of refrain with which they try to laugh at what cannot be helped.

It is only in the farewell scene in the "cool shade of her little Dutch-looking dining-room" (II, 319) that Maria comes any nearer to being explicit about her own feeling, saying when he calls her apartment a haunt of peace " 'I wish with all my heart . . . I could make you treat it as a haven of rest.' On which they fronted each other, across the table, as if things unuttered were in the air" (II, 320). James brings them even nearer to utterance when he makes her declare:

"There's nothing, you know, I would n't do for you."

"Oh yes—I know."

"There's nothing," she repeated, "in all the world."

"I know, I know. But all the same I must go. . . . To be right" (II, 326).

And so, having admirably served both James's purpose and Strether's because she has so much of "the dignity of a prime idea," she is left to face Strether's departure.

She sighed it at last, all comically, all tragically, away. "I can't indeed resist you."

"Then there we are!" said Strether (II, 327).

VI ~ "The Troubled Life Mostly at the Centre of Our Subject"

The characters who are centers of consciousness in James's fiction are inevitably the central focus of his presentation of the mingled tragedy and comedy of life. "The possible other case" for them is always implied—and always impossible. James accentuates awareness of the comedy which is really tragic by all degrees of serious single-mindedness or capacity for comic judgment on the part of the central characters themselves. With Maisie's earnest incomprehension of what she "knows" at one end and Strether's ironic self-mockery at the other, he suggests the whole spectrum of possible kinds of sensitivity to the incongruities which are the essence of the given situation. His free spirits are all people who, "affected with a certain high lucidity, thereby become characters; in consequence of which their doings, their sufferings or whatever, take on . . . an importance" (*The Art of the Novel,* p. 130). It is of Fleda Vetch, Laura Wing, and Rose Tramore that James is speaking when he establishes this criterion of importance,

and he lists "acuteness and intensity, reflexion and passion," as their "attributes and advantages." He immediately puts these "very young women" in a larger company: "They are thus of a family—which shall have also for us, we seem forewarned, more members, and of each sex" (*The Art of the Novel*, p. 130). The family, indeed, includes practically all of James's main characters, for it was his conviction that "the figures in any picture, the agents in any drama, are interesting only in proportion as they feel their respective situations" (*The Art of the Novel*, p. 62). One of the most striking variations in this family resemblance of lucidity is in the degree of comic perception it includes. What makes the plight of Nanda Brookenham peculiarly moving is the absolute clarity with which she sees the truth and the high generosity with which she accepts it; but her perception is totally serious and straightforward.[1] Hyacinth Robinson feels bitterly the irony of his situation: the incongruity of his nature and his circumstances is the sharpest fact of his consciousness even before he becomes embroiled with Paul Muniment and the Princess. But exactly one of the ironies which increases his suffering is that he is incapable of any objective view of it. Lambert Strether, on the other hand, has so marked a degree of comic detachment that it would hardly seem credible except for his being more than twice the age of Nanda or Hyacinth. Different as these three characters are in their sense of comedy, the lucidity of each is what most brings out the essence of the cruel joke played on them by the combination of their particular sensibilities and the conditions in which they must act.

The somber beauty of Nanda Brookenham's high seriousness is increased by the frivolity of the world in which she moves. Even the method of *The Awkward Age*

1. *The Awkward Age* is, of course, one of the novels in which James uses more than one center of consciousness; but Nanda is the one who most engages sympathy, and she is the most central since she is at the center of the problem on which they all throw light.

is that of drawing room comedy; and it is of all James's works of fiction the one in which he was most conscious of submitting to the rigors of the dramatic method. "Each of my 'lamps' would be the light of a single 'social occasion.' . . . The beauty of the conception was in this approximation of the respective divisions of my form to the successive Acts of a Play" (*The Art of the Novel*, p. 110). In the brilliance of the dialogue of the successive social occasions, James suggests not only the wit of Congreve but something of the social milieu of Restoration comedy.[2] In the Preface he makes one of his frequent apologies for letting a work exceed the limits he had set for it: "I say all, surely, when I speak of the thing as planned, in perfect good faith, for brevity, for levity, for simplicity, for jocosity, in fine, and for an accomodating [sic] irony" (*The Art of the Novel*, p. 98). The levity of the world in which conversation grows "bad" (*The Awkward Age*, p. 284) when any curb of delicacy must be placed on subjects of gossip is fully conveyed. But it is precisely the free tone of the repartee in Mrs. Brook's drawing room which makes the situation of Nanda "impossible" and tragic.[3]

In the verbal fencing between Mrs. Brookenham and the Duchess the thrusts which they level at each other under the cover of clever politeness are as nasty as any in *The Way of the World*. The antipathy between them is evident in their opposite social techniques. The Duchess, who makes a great point of being shocked at the way

2. In 1888, James wrote to Stevenson: "Edmund Gosse has sent me his clever little life of Congreve, just out, and I have read it—but it isn't so good as his Raleigh. But no more was the insufferable subject" [*The Letters of Henry James*, ed. Percy Lubbock (New York, 1920), I, 138]. His finding Congreve insufferable gives added emphasis to his own sense of all the tragic life underneath the drama of manners. This awareness of what goes on below the brilliant social surface is as present in his fiction as it is absent from Restoration comedy.

3. "For *The Awkward Age*, though it exhibits James's genius for social comedy at its most brilliant, is a tragedy; a tragedy conceived in an imagination that was robustly, delicately and clairvoyantly moral" [F. R. Leavis, *The Great Tradition* (London, 1948), p. 170].

Nanda, as an unmarried girl, is allowed to know what
goes on, has guarded her niece, little Aggie, "to create a
particular little rounded and tinted innocence . . . deliberately prepared for consumption" (p. 238). Malicious as
she is, Mrs. Brook is telling the truth when she says, "Aggie,
don't you see? is the Duchess's morality, her virtue; which,
by having it that way outside of you, as one may say, you
can make a much better thing of" (p. 310). The Duchess'
affairs and her present pursuit of Lord Petherton, who lives
off the accommodating Mitchy, are notorious; whereas the
Duchess, in the course of making clear to Mr. Longdon that
Mrs. Brookenham "wants 'old Van' for herself" (p. 253) and
is thus the chief obstacle to Nanda's marrying Van, has
to assure him that Mrs. Brook and Van "have n't done,
as it's called, anything wrong" (p. 402). These two pursue
their rival purposes with an enmity the more apparent for
being not quite openly acknowledged; and the women
Mrs. Brook befriends lead no more savory lives. She is the
general confidante and counselor of wives who are involved
in adulterous love affairs; and her "helping" them is all
part of her notion of amusement. In the midst of her
supposed efforts to keep Lady Fanny from "bolting," when
Van asks, "But why not let her go?" she can declare, "She 's
the delight of our life. . . . She 's the ornament of our
circle, . . . She will, she won't—she won't she will! It 's the
excitement, every day, of plucking the daisy over" (p. 178).
Lady Fanny, the sister of the worthless Lord Petherton, is
too blank a creature, "magnificent, simple, stupid" (p. 107),
to arouse much concern over the frivolous entertainment at
her expense; but what makes the conversation sinister is
that it has been introduced by Van's protest at Nanda's
exposure to the advances of Cashmore, Lady Fanny's
bounder of a husband, and Mrs. Brook has discussed her
own daughter's involvement in these sordid affairs with the
same casual interest in a guessing game. She is glad to
have Nanda save Mrs. Donner from Cashmore because,
"If Carrie *is* rescued it 's a pretext the less for Fanny" (p.

178), to go off with Captain Dent-Douglas. She is equally
unconcerned when shortly afterward it seems to be her son
Harold who is keeping Fanny contentedly in London.
Indeed the shifts of entanglements become so involved that
it is hard at a given moment to tell who is in danger of
"bolting" with whom. Little Aggie, as soon as Nanda gets
Mitchy to marry her, plunges into the freedoms of the
world with such a splash that she immediately steals Petherton from her aunt; and apparently their only reason for
not going off together is that both continue to live on
Mitchy's bounty.

This is the world into which Nanda is projected,
brought down from the nursery to "sit" in her mother's
drawing room, of which the Duchess gives Mr. Longdon an
accurate account as she explains why Nanda must marry
promptly if she is not to be too battered to marry at all.
She says of Mrs. Brook:

> But she's amusing—highly amusing. I do her perfect
> justice. As your women go she 's rare. If she were
> French she 'd be a *femme d'esprit*. She has invented
> a *nuance* of her own and she has done it all by
> herself, for Edward figures in her drawingroom only
> as one of those queer extinguishers of fire in the
> corridors of hotels. He 's just a bucket on a peg.
> The men, the young and the clever ones, find it a
> house—and heaven knows they 're right—with intel-
> lectual elbow-room, with freedom of talk. Most Eng-
> lish talk is a quadrille in a sentry-box. You'll tell me
> we go further in Italy, and I won't deny it, but in
> Italy we have the common sense not to have little
> girls in the room. The young men hang about Mrs.
> Brook, and the clever ones ply her with the uproar-
> ious appreciation that keeps her up to the mark.
> She 's in a prodigious fix—she must sacrifice either
> her daughter or what she once called to me her
> intellectual habits. Mr. Vanderbank, you 've seen
> for yourself, is one of the most cherished, the most
> confirmed. Three months ago—it could n't any
> longer be kept off—Nanda began definitely to 'sit';

to be there and look, by the tea-table, modestly and conveniently abstracted (p. 255).

The degree of Nanda's difference from this world is marked by old Mr. Longdon's devotion to her, a devotion initiated by her resemblance to her grandmother whom he has loved ever since his own youth, but turning gradually into a cherishing of the girl's own special beauty of being. Her young gravity matches his old-fashioned formality; and the two move with the dignity of a kind of quiet saraband among the whirling figures who surround them. They are the only two major characters who are free from pose, though Mitchy is equally lovable in his pose of self-mocking clown. When Nanda is introduced at Van's intimate tea party for Mr. Longdon, she answers Mitchy's sally about her having possibly come on a bicycle with perfect literalness: "No, I walked" (p. 131). She offers with a "faint quaver" (p. 132) to make tea, explaining that her mother has told her to offer and taught her that morning how to do it. In deference both to her and to Mr. Longdon, Mitchy and Van try to brush over her intimacy with Tishy Grendon, the sister of the compromised Mrs. Donner, and Van says,

. . . "Don't believe a word of anything of the sort."

He had spoken as with the intention of a large vague optimism; but there was plainly something in the girl that would always make for lucidity. "Do you mean about Carrie Donner? I *don't* believe it, and at any rate I don't think it's any one's business. I should n't have a very high opinion of a person who would give up a friend" (pp. 136-37). James explains that there is neither pertness nor passion in her speech; but that it might well have perplexed Mr. Longdon "to see her at once so downright as from experience and yet of so fresh and sweet a tenderness of youth" (p. 137). When Mr. Longdon rushes from the room overwhelmed by her resemblance to her grandmother, the beautiful Lady Julia, and Van follows him, she is left

alone with Mitchy. That her simplicity is the opposite of
imperception is demonstrated by the delicacy with which
she lets Mitchy know how much she likes him, and that
her mother has told her of his asking rather hopelessly and
ironically for her hand. His answering with his usual
bantering self-mockery does not obscure the seriousness
with which he declares, "But I adore you, all the same,
without illusions." Her consciousness of her own plight
comes out vividly in her rejoinder: "Don't 'adore' a girl,
Mr. Mitchy—just help her. That 's more to the purpose"
(p. 140). And so he does throughout the novel do his
best to help, even to the point of marrying Aggie to get
himself out of the way lest his simply being available
should prevent a proposal from Van, on whom all the
ardor of Nanda's passion is fixed. His own suffering, which
he masks with laughter, makes him a fitting person to
enlighten Van, who has sent Nanda to speak to Mr. Longdon.

    Mitchy, on the sofa, received with meditation a
light. "Will she understand? She has everything in the
world but one," he added. "But that 's half."

    Vanderbank, before him, lighted for himself. "What
is it?"

    "A sense of humour."

    "Oh yes, she 's serious."

    Mitchy smoked a little. "She 's tragic" (pp. 142-43).

    After this announcement of her direction, James
lets her move through the whole tragic rhythm of passion,
purpose, perception, befriended only by Mr. Longdon, the
relic of an earlier age, and Mitchy, who is so grotesquely
ugly that he dresses in violently mismatched garments so
that "the effect of comedy might not escape him if secured
by a real plunge" (p. 78). Near the end of the novel Mr.
Longdon says to Mitchy:

    . . . "But if Nanda did n't trust us, . . . her case
would indeed be a sorry one. She has nobody else to trust."

"Yes." Mitchy's concurrence was grave. "Only you and me."

"Only you and me" (pp. 480-81).

Her mother's brittle world of high comedy is not only the source of her tragedy in exposing her to knowledge which Van cannot tolerate in a girl who is to become his wife; it is also the setting against which her suffering must be borne except when Mr. Longdon takes her to the quiet of his home at Beccles. This incongruity is the constant accentuation of what she must bear, both emphasizing by contrast her gallantly hidden pain and actually making her plight steadily worse as she is more and more exposed to the knowledge Van finds deplorable. She knows "everything." "But of course she can't help it, . . . Everything, literally everything, in London, in the world she lives in, is in the air she breathes—so that the longer *she*'s in it the more she'll know" (p. 378). Yet Van cannot quite bring himself to rescue her, though he tries because he "wants to be kind" and because he wants both for Nanda and for himself the fortune Mr. Longdon has offered to settle on her if she marries Van. Twice James presents him poised to speak, almost uttering a proposal and then drawing back. "The trouble is" as he says to Mitchy, who has declared that too much knowledge matters only for the girls on whom no one takes pity, "that it's just a thing that may sometimes operate as a bar to pity. Is n't it for the non-marrying girls that it does n't particularly matter? For the others it's such an odd preparation" (p. 378).

The conversation takes place just before the party at Tishy Grendon's, where Mrs. Brookenham, with a special glitter in her eye, sets about finally showing Van that the preparation is impossible and so horrifying Mr. Longdon that he will be led to "adopt" Nanda in order to rescue her permanently from such a life. This scene in which, as Van later tells her, she pulls them all down "just closing with each of the great columns in its turn—as Samson pulled down the temple" (p. 439), is her most

triumphant comic performance; and it is exactly the boldness of the comedy which makes it the crisis of Nanda's
tragedy. Mrs. Brookenham arranges the stage and gathers
about her all the other players except Petherton and Aggie,
who are engaged in a "romp," an actual physical tussle,
in the adjoining room over possession of a French novel,
which Petherton is supposedly trying to wrest from Aggie
to protect her from reading it. Mrs. Brook launches in
with the direct question to Mr. Longdon, "Why do you
hate me so?" (p. 407). But her directness is as much a
pose, a move in her game, as is the politeness with which
she cloaks her witty insults to the Duchess about Aggie
and Petherton or parries the Duchess' to her about Harold's
infatuating Lady Fanny. Along the way she has brought
in mocking references to Mrs. Donner and to Tishy Grendon's broken nose, a phrase which Vanderbank has to
explain to Mr. Longdon: . . . "Mr. Grendon does n't like
her." The addition of these words apparently made the difference—as if they constituted a fresh link with the irresistible comedy of things. That he was unexpectedly di-
verting was, however, no check to Mr. Longdon's deliver-
ing his full thought. "Very horrid of two sisters to be both,
in their marriages, so wretched" (p. 412).

After Mrs. Brook's announcement to Mr. Longdon
that he must give Nanda back, the Duchess takes pains to
ask Mr. Brookenham when he joins the group if they do
want Nanda. " 'Want' her, Jane? We would n't *take* her"
(p. 418). The Duchess makes the most of this revelation
of domestic misunderstanding; but her sparring seems only
to inspire Mrs. Brookenham to new flights of witty malice
about Aggie and Petherton, while Mitchy sitting "with
head dropped and knees pressing his hands together," says
to Harold, "I don't mind any one's saying anything" (p.
427).

Tishy has come out with the fact that Aggie is sitting
on the novel; so when the romping pair reappear, Mrs.

Brook greets them with: . . . "See—he *has* pulled her off!" . . .

Little Aggie, to whom plenty of pearls were singularly becoming, met it as pleasant sympathy. "Yes, and it was a *real* pull. But of course," she continued with the prettiest humour and as if Mrs. Brook would quite understand, "from the moment one has a person's nails, and almost his teeth, in one's flesh—!" (p. 431).

This offers a perfect opportunity for Mrs. Brook to exclaim over the prints in Aggie's arms. Through all the demolition of her mother's targets, Nanda has been silent; but when Harold discovers Van's name on the cover of the objectionable book, Nanda, with her usual forthrightness, explains that she has put it there when she brought the book into the house.

. . . "Have you read this work, Nanda?"

"Yes mamma."

"Oh I say!" cried Mr. Cashmore, hilarious and turning the leaves.

Mr. Longdon had by this time ceremoniously approached Tishy. "Good-night" (p. 434).

After this, both comedy and tragedy are complete. All that remains is the denouement in which the full beauty of Nanda's character is revealed. Her clarity of vision has throughout been one of her strengths. She has from childhood seen things without being told; and she understands her situation as clearly as do any of the older people who deplore it for her. In the conversation with Mr. Longdon at Mertle when she is discussing his acceptance of her difference from her grandmother, she says: "If we 're both partly the result of other people, *her* other people were so different. . . . Granny was n't the kind of girl she *could* n't be—and so neither am I." (pp. 230-31). And she sees with equal clarity what this means about her marrying the only man she can love. When Mr. Longdon expresses the wish that she would marry, she states quite simply the fact that: "It 's lovely of you to wish it, but I shall be one

of the people who don't. I shall be at the end . . . **one** of those who have n't" (p. 232). Again in the conversation with Mitchy at Beccles when she is urging him to save Aggie by marrying her and removing her from the atmosphere of the Duchess, she says, "but my situation, my exposure—all the results of them I show. Does n't one become a sort of little drain-pipe with everything flowing through? . . . Well, it sticks to us. And that 's what you don't mind!" (p. 358). But the man she could love would mind; and when Mitchy desolately points this out and asks, "Do you positively *like* to love in vain?" She answers, "Yes" (p. 359). Finally, at the beginning of the disastrous evening at Tishy Grendon's before the other guests arrive, she says to Van himself, "Oh it's all over . . . my little hour. And the danger of picking up" (p. 388). Thus James has shown her gradually building the courage to face what everyone except Mr. Longdon really recognizes and Mrs. Brookenham repeatedly declares: that Van "won't do it." He has led straight to the judgment of the two who love her. Mitchy says to Mr. Longdon:

> . . . "With Nanda . . . it *is* deep."
> His companion took it from him. "Deep."
> "And yet somehow it is n't abject."
> The old man wondered. " 'Abject'?"
> "I mean it is n't pitiful. In its way," Mitchy developed, "it's happy."
> This too, though rather ruefully, Mr. Longdon could take from him. "Yes—in its way."
> "Any passion so great, so complete," Mitchy went on, "is—satisfied or unsatisfied—a life" (pp. 481-82).

The last book of the novel, which bears Nanda's name, simply rounds out and makes more rich the impression of her tragic dignity which Mitchy has announced on her first appearance and which has grown as she has grown through the long experience crowded into the short months covered by the novel. The "social occasion" which

James picks for this final demonstration is beautifully appropriate, as she dispenses tea and a way of dealing with the situation to each in turn of the three men she cares about. She lets Van splutter on in his embarrassment just long enough and then relieves his mind by asking him to become again an habitué of her mother's drawing room. Mitchy too she asks to go to see her mother; but the help she gives him is the feeling that she knows what he is suffering from Aggie and the promise never to abandon him. What she must do for Mr. Longdon, who is coming to learn her decision about being "adopted" by him, is harder: to convince him that there is no hope of Van's changing. After Mr. Longdon's anger at Van's having asked her to make his apologies has a little subsided, the old man says to her: "It would be good for me—by which I mean it would be easier for me—if you did n't quite so immensely care for him. . . . so wonderfully love him" (pp. 539-40). And protesting that she does n't, she collapses in a torrent of tears. "Her buried face could only after a moment give way to the flood, and she sobbed in a passion as sharp and brief as the flurry of a wild thing for an instant uncaged" (p. 540). But for all her momentary breaking down, she manages to get said to him that her reason for inviting Van to tea "was that—with whatever idea you had—you should see for yourself how he could come and go. . . . Here he was. I did n't care what he thought. Here I brought him. And his reasons remain" (p. 542). A little later she goes on, "I *am* like that. . . . Like what he thinks." When Mr. Longdon acknowledges that he does know what she means, she asks, "Well?" and his answer is, "Well!" "He raised his hands and took her face, which he drew so close to his own that, as she gently let him, he could kiss her with solemnity on the forehead. 'Come!' he then very firmly said—quite indeed as if it were a question of their moving on the spot" (p. 543).

Shortly after the first meeting with Mr. Longdon, Nanda has declared to Van, " 'I shall never change—I shall

always be just the same. The same old mannered modern slangy hack,' she continued quite gravely. 'Mr. Longdon has made me feel that. . . . I 'm about as good as I can be —and about as bad. If Mr. Longdon can't make me different nobody can' " (p. 214). This is part of the directness that makes "her honesty almost violent" (p. 149). But for all the demonstration of her candor in Nanda's own statement, Mitchy's comment voices the deeper truth of her nature: "Nanda . . . to the end of all her time, will simply remain exquisite, or genuine, or generous—whatever we choose to call it" (p. 307).[4]

∼   ∼   ∼

The world of Hyacinth Robinson, the little book-binder who sprang up, James says, "out of the London pavement" (*The Art of the Novel*, p. 60), is as different as possible from the drawing room comedy atmosphere which creates and then steadily intensifies the tragedy of Nanda Brookenham. But for him too the circumstances in which he is placed are the essence of cruel incongruity.

4. The plight of the sensitive young person, who "knows" encompassing evil without being corrupted by it seems always to have engaged James's sympathy. In both "The Pupil" and *What Maisie Knew* he treats the surrounding baseness with satiric comedy and poignantly renders the suffering which the comic characters cause the children. In the *Notebooks*, he speaks of the "melancholy comedy," "the ugly little comedy," (pp. 262-63) in which Maisie is involved. But in the Preface he says that the "appearances in themselves vulgar and empty enough . . . become, as she deals with them, the stuff of poetry and tragedy and art" (*The Art of the Novel*, p. 147). The similarity in the kind of suffering which their elders inflict on Morgan and Maisie is suggested in the Notebook entry where James records the germ from which he evolved the later story and tells himself to make the child a girl "which would make it different from *The Pupil*" (*Notebooks*, p. 126). The two stories are placed together in the New York Edition as stories of the "troubled vision" of young observers. But moving as are these children betrayed by their elders and by the very manners of the adult world in which they move, they do not attain the fullness of tragic stature which James gives to Nanda.

In the account of his origins, James goes to melodramatic lengths to supply reasons for his difference both from Pinnie, the tiny dressmaker who strives so earnestly to bring him up as a little gentleman, and from the other more sordid inhabitants of the miserable Lomax Place, where she takes lodgers "of such a class that they were not always to be depended upon to settle her weekly account [and has] a strain to make two ends meet, for all the sign between her windows—

MISS AMANDA PYNSENT
Modes et Robes

DRESSMAKING IN ALL ITS BRANCHES: COURTDRESSES: MANTLES AND FASHIONABLE BONNETS (*The Princess Casamassima*, I, 34).

The opening scene of the novel is the comical one of Pinnie's being overawed by the powerful Mrs. Bowerbank, who while she sociably consumes brandy—kept by Pinnie for emergencies and now produced with hot water and sugar for this occasion "of a highly exceptional kind" (I, 4)—regales poor Pinnie with the story of her coming from prison to bring the dying request of Hyacinth's mother to see her child. Broad as is the comedy with which James presents Mrs. Bowerbank, "a high-shouldered, towering woman [who] suggested squareness as well as a pervasion of the upper air, so that Amanda reflected that she must be very difficult to fit, and had a sinking at the idea of the number of pins she would take," (I, 7), she confronts the tender-hearted Pinnie with the insoluble problem of whether to expose the child to the frightening experience of visiting the prison. What most frightens Pinnie herself is the possibility, which she obscurely feels as a certainty, of his beginning thus to learn of his being the illegitimate son of a French girl named Florentine, whom Pinnie has known when they were in service together, and presumably of Lord Purvis, whom the passionate girl has murdered for deserting her. The tone of Mrs. Bowerbank's "official pessimism" is ludicrous when she makes the pro-

nouncement: "There's one thing you may be sure of: whatever you decide to do, as soon as ever he grows up he'll make you wish you had done the opposite" (I, 14). She has, however, given the clue not only to Pinnie's desolating predicament but also to the dilemma of Hyacinth's dislocation. Since he belongs neither to the world of his mother nor to that of his supposed father, and still less to that of the respectable little dressmaker, there is no course of action which will not suggest that its opposite might have been better. Pinnie's hints of his grand lineage and her assurance that he has the nature and bearing of an aristocrat are one way in which the anomaly of the child's growing up in Lomax Place is emphasized; Pinnie's romantic view of Hyacinth is used in somewhat the same way as are Susan Stringham's constant references to Milly as a Princess in *The Wings of the Dove*. James's tender mockery both undercuts and makes convincing the sentimentality of the two adoring older women. At the same time, just as the insistent references to her as Princess make both the reader and the girl herself see Milly in that rôle, so here Pinnie's reiterated innuendos about Hyacinth's high birth fix the idea indelibly in the mind of the boy and operate on the reader as a steady reminder of his complicated inheritance.

The reality with which Hyacinth exists as a person establishes the authenticity of his strange background and his present suffering. James says in the Preface that: "'Subjects' and situations, character and history, the tragedy and comedy of life, are things of which the common air, in such conditions [his perambulation of the London streets] seems pungently to taste" (*The Art of the Novel*, p. 59). But however acute the suffering of a tormented and deprived young person condemned to view all the accumulations of civilization only from the outside, "the interest of the attitude and the act would be the actor's imagination and vision of them, together with the nature and degree of their felt return upon him" (*The Art of*

the Novel, p. 63). And so he creates Hyacinth with a "consciousness . . . subject to fine intensification and wide enlargement" (*The Art of the Novel,* p. 67). At the same time, he reminds himself, as he frequently does in the Prefaces, that: "If persons either tragically or comically embroiled with life allow us the comic or tragic value of their embroilment in proportion as their struggle is a measured and directed one, it is strangely true, none the less, that beyond a certain point they are spoiled for us by this carrying of a due light" (*The Art of the Novel,* p. 63). The bewilderment of the hero is essential to the interest; but "the whole thing comes to depend thus on the *quality* of the bewilderment characteristic of one's creature" (*The Art of the Novel,* p. 66).

James shows Hyacinth as finely bewildered from the first picture of him standing before the sweet-shop spelling out the front pages of the romances displayed in the windows and then spending only half his penny on stale lollipops in order to have half for a ballad with a woodcut at the top, until the final scene when the Princess and Schinkel break into his room and find that he has killed himself with the bullet intended for the Duke. At every stage of his life he is pulled in two directions. An evening at the pantomime, to which Mr. Vetch has provided tickets, is enchantment for Hyacinth. "There were things in life of which, even at the age of ten, it was a conviction of the boy's that it would be his fate never to see enough, and one of these was the wonder-world illuminated by those playhouse lamps" (I, 23). After Hyacinth has become a bookbinder, thanks again to the good offices of Mr. Vetch in getting him apprenticed to the skillful Mr. Crookendon, he is taken up by "the awful little 'Enning" (I, 60), now a full-blown beauty of a model in a shop near Buckingham Palace. The description of him at this point ends: "There was something exotic in him, and yet, with his sharp young face, destitute of bloom but not of sweetness, and a certain conscious cockneyism that pervaded him,

he was as strikingly as Millicent, in her own degree, a product of the London streets and the London air. He looked both ingenuous and slightly wasted, amused, amusing and indefinably sad. Women had always found him touching, but he made them—so they had repeatedly assured him—die of laughing" (I, 79-80). As he roams the streets with Millicent Henning or even indulges her taste for beer or prawns, her hearty good will and simple conceit give him both excitement and reassurance, even while he is repelled by her vulgarity. "If she had been ugly he could n't have listened to her; but the rare bloom and grand style of her person glorified even her accent, interfused her cockney genius with prismatic hues, gave her a large and constant impunity" (I, 165). Though his skillful fellow worker, the emigré Poupin, and the power-driven young chemical worker, Paul Muniment, have interested him in revolutionary activity which at some vague time in the future will overthrow the privileged classes, and Hyacinth sometimes amuses himself by picturing Millicent as a revolutionary figure inspiring resistance at such a barricade as the one where his French grandfather had perished, he is no more single-minded in his views of society than in his views of the cockney beauty.

> The sense of privation with her was often extremely acute; but she could always put her finger on the remedy. With her fellow-sufferer the case was very different; the remedy for him was terribly vague and inaccessible. He was liable to moods in which the sense of exclusion from all he would have liked most to enjoy in life settled on him like a pall. They had a bitterness, but they were not invidious—they were not moods of vengeance, of imaginary spoilation: they were simply states of paralysing melancholy, . . . Everything which in a great city could touch the sentient faculty of a youth on whom nothing was lost ministered to his conviction that there was no possible good fortune in life of too 'quiet' an order for him to appreciate—no privilege, no opportunity, no luxury to which he might n't do full

justice. It was not so much that he wanted to enjoy as that he wanted to know; his desire was n't to be pampered but to be initiated (I, 168-69).

His initiation comes just after he has committed himself by a solemn vow to do a task, whatever will be required of him by the revolutionaries, which will probably mean his own death. James ties the knot of ironies as tight as possible by letting the instrument of his initiation be the Princess Casamassima, who has the worthless Captain Sholto pick Hyacinth up for her as a specimen of the lower classes. For all her beauty and wealth and position, she is as bewildered in her unhappiness as is Hyacinth himself and is now trying to assuage her restlessness by helping the "people." Since she is simply the most beautiful woman in Europe and can be the most gracious, it is no wonder that Hyacinth falls completely under her spell, yielding absolutely first to the bedazzlement of her personal splendor and then to all the grace of civilized life with which she surrounds him at Medley. His walk in the gardens before breakfast "was peopled with recognitions; he had been dreaming all his life of just such a place and such objects, such a morning and such a chance. . . . There was something in the way the grey walls rose from the green lawn that brought tears to his eyes" (II, 7). After she has taken him over the great house, she does make some apology for its grandeur. "It must appear to him so preposterous for a woman to associate herself with the great uprising of the poor and yet live in palatial halls" (II, 17-18). Spellbound as Hyacinth is, he has not so completely lost his sense of humor as to be "unconscious of the anomaly she mentioned. It had been present to him all day; it added much to the way life practised on his sense of the tragi-comical to think of the Princess's having retired to a private paradise to think out the problem of the slums" (II, 18). Yet hollow-sounding as are her professions about preferring simplicity and taking the place only because it was cheap and "wretched" (II, 19), she

means them to the extent of giving up both Medley and her grand house in London, as soon as she has thrown cord after cord of her net around Hyacinth to bind him not only to herself but to the cherishableness of all the deposits of ancient beauty and civilization which Medley represents. James uses both his own direct satire and Madame Grandoni's sardonic comments to show how much of play acting there is in Christina's adopting the simple life in the small house she has taken in Madeira Crescent, which for all its hideousness, is comfortable enough to seem "lovely" (II, 230) to Paul Muniment. But her retaining at least the maid Assunta and the Italian cook from her old menage and her having kept some of her treasures in storage do not reduce for Hyacinth the shock of finding her in the midst "of so much that was common and ugly" (II, 177). He has come back from Paris and Venice, where the good Mr. Vetch has sent him to recover from Pinnie's death and to be weaned from revolutionary commitments, less than ever desirous to destroy society. "What was supreme in his mind to-day was not the idea of how the society that surrounded him should be destroyed; it was much more the sense of the wonderful precious things it had produced, of the fabric of beauty and power it had raised" (II, 124-25). During his wistful mediations in Paris, he has already come to see something of the callousness with which Paul Muniment has sacrificed his trusting friend to the revolutionaries; and now he must watch as the Princess, growing more and more embroiled in the excitement of plots and stratagems, discards him for Paul, who cares only for the money she can supply and uses her as ruthlessly as he has used Hyacinth. She treats Hyacinth kindly; and in answer to his question, "Have n't you kept *anything?*" She answers, "I 've kept *you*" (II, 174). This is true enough. He felt that: "No adventure was so prodigious as sticking as fast as possible to *her*" (II, 163). But he at last perceives all too clearly that she no longer takes him seriously and knows as well as if he had heard her say it

to Paul that she regards him as "foolish" and "deplorably conventional" (II, 295).

And so, just after he has made up his mind that "the world 's an awfully jolly place" (II, 154), he begins the painfully solitary approach to the fulfillment of his vow. James shows his isolation by the account of Sunday excursions with Paul, whom he vainly taxes for the first time with want of feeling, and with Milly, who treats him with unprecedented warmth of affection after hearing the story of his birth and then puts him off for the evening by a flimsy excuse of having to visit her forewoman, which lets him know that she is going to join Sholto. When, seeking anyhow to avoid solitude, he goes to see Lady Aurora, he feels nearer to her than ever before; but it is the communion of desolation: "What had each done but lose that which he or she had never so much as had?" (II, 354). Still unable to bear his own company, he goes on to see the Poupins in Lisson Grove and finds there the German revolutionary Schinkel. He at once senses the uneasy atmosphere and finally demands of Schinkel what he has to tell him.

"Why should I have anything to tell you?" Schinkel almost whined.

"I don't know that—yet I believe you have. I make out things, I guess things quickly. That 's my nature at all times, and I do it much more now" (II, 367). It is this acuteness of sensibility which has steadily exacerbated the torment with which Hyacinth has experienced the whole succession of ironies. He must face still another when the Poupins in their distress and bewilderment say that since he has ceased to believe in the people, he has no right to act for them. His answer is, "Does it alter my sacred vow? There are some things in which one can't change. I did n't promise to believe; I promised to obey" (II, 371). It is in this frame of mind that he finally receives from Schinkel the fatal letter ordering him to kill the Duke within the next few days.

James shows him then in a series of encounters which strip away any last hope of sympathetic understanding. The alarmed visit of the devoted Mr. Vetch simply gives him the task of assuaging the old man's fears. In Madeira Crescent he finds the Princess at first kind, but abstracted, and then exalted by a passionate affirmation of her own commitment to the cause. "That she had done with him, done with him for ever, was to remain the most vivid impression Hyacinth had carried away from Madeira Crescent" (II, 418). When he goes out next morning, sick with the horror of the bloody deed to be done, "London had never appeared to him to wear more proudly and publicly the stamp of her imperial history" (II, 420). In his longing for comfort, he seeks out Millicent Henning in her haberdasher's establishment, against her express prohibition of visits there; "and though he hovered a long time, undecided, embarrassed, half-ashamed, at last he went in as by the force of the one, the last, sore personal need left him. He would just make an appointment with her, and a glance of the eye and a single word would suffice" (II, 422). The glance he meets is that of Captain Sholto, before whom Milly is posturing as she shows off the latest creation of the shop; so Hyacinth turns away without her knowing of his presence.

It is small wonder that James chooses the Preface to *The Princess Casamassima* to make the declaration that "the gross fools, the headlong fools, the fatal fools . . . are apt largely indeed, on a near view, to be all the cause of [the trouble for the consciousness] subject to fine intensification and wide enlargement" (*The Art of the Novel*, p. 67). Hyacinth has been surrounded by a variety of fools who as they play out their comedy create his tragedy.

～　　　～　　　～

Hyacinth's acute perception of the ironies of his existence breaks out from time to time in flights of cynical

humor; but his consciousness is too tormented to let him
see any of his experience as comic. Just as for Nanda
Brookenham, it is the impinging of the incongruities of
comedy from the world around him which emphasizes his
plight. But in *The Ambassadors,* James gives to Lambert
Strether the power to see himself as a comic figure; and
it is this faculty of detached judgment of his own frustra-
tions which paradoxically most intensifies them. It is, in
fact, his habit of self-scrutiny out of which his dilemmas
arise. In the first excursion with Maria at Chester when
he keeps looking at his watch and she taxes him with
doing something he thinks not right, his ability to laugh at
himself and his actually overdeveloped conscience both
come out in his droll response: "Am I enjoying it as much
as *that?*" (*The Ambassadors,* I, 16). His gradual discarding
of the standards of Woollett, Massachusetts, makes much
of the progress of the novel; but he is already capable of
judging them objectively when he tells Maria: "Woollett
is n't sure it ought to enjoy" (I, 16). Under Miss Gostrey's
tutelage, he does learn to enjoy; but he always stands off
and sees himself doing it, and he never outgrows his New
England conscience.

After a morning's enchanted stroll along the rue de
la Paix, through the Tuileries Gardens, and by the river,
he sits in the Luxembourg Gardens pondering the effect
of his first week in Europe: "Everything he wanted was
comprised moreover in a single boon—the common unattainable art of taking things as they came. He appeared
to himself to have given his best years to an active appreciation of the way they did n't come; but perhaps—as they
would seemingly here be things quite other—this long ache
might at last drop to rest" (I, 83). Instead, the ache increases as he feels the successive impressions of the beauty
of Paris itself, of the transformation of Chad from a boor
to a charming man of the world, and finally of the revelation at the great scene in Gloriani's garden that the woman
from whose evil influence Mrs. Newsome has sent him to

rescue her son is the epitome of all the grace of the old civilization which has enthralled him. It is the Woollett standards of rectitude which make him cling so desperately to Little Bilham's lie that the relation between Chad and Madame de Vionnet is a "virtuous attachment" (I, 180). He feels himself as pompous and priggish; but he still asks Chad, "Is her life without reproach?" (I, 239). It is his sense of duty again that makes him insist to Madame de Vionnet, just when he is falling more completely in love with her after the encounter in Notre Dame, that it is time for him to go home now that he has put the case to Chad and "had, as we say at Woollett, a lovely time" (II, 20). But even as he insists, he knows that he is lost.

> What had come over him as he recognised her in the nave of the church was that holding off could be but a losing game from the instant she was worked for not only by her subtlety, but by the hand of fate itself. If all the accidents were to fight on her side—and by the actual showing they loomed large— he could only give himself up. This was what he had done in privately deciding then and there to propose she should breakfast with him. What did the success of his proposal in fact resemble but the smash in which a regular runaway properly ends? The smash was their walk, their déjeuner, their omelette, the Chablis, the place, the view, their present talk and his present pleasure in it—to say nothing, wonder of wonders, of her own. To this tune and nothing less, accordingly, was his surrender made good (II, 14-15).

In every step of his surrender, he stands off and sees himself surrendering. He has long ago explained to Maria, "I 'm always considering something else; something else, I mean, than the thing of the moment" (I, 19). This double view constantly complicates and intensifies his present experience, as it does strikingly in the scene where he perceives that Madame de Vionnet is "giving him over to ruin" (II, 92) by her show of intimacy with him before Sarah Pocock. He feels keenly how much she is wrecking his

future relation with the new emissary from Woollett; yet he feels all the comedy of the social fencing between the two women. Later he even condemns his agitation as "pusillanimous"; but "he recognised once more the perverse law that so inveterately governed his poor personal aspects: it would be exactly *like* the way things always turned out for him that he should affect Mrs. Pocock and Waymarsh as launched in a relation in which he had really never been launched at all" (II, 94).

This power to stand off and see his "poor personal aspects" is partly what enables him to assuage his conscience as he succumbs to the charm of Madame de Vionnet and changes sides in the battle for Chad. Deeply engaged as his feelings are, he tells himself that he is not directly involved. He comforts himself by "clinging again intensely to the strength of his position, which was precisely that there was nothing in it for himself" (II, 60). It is the feeling of consistency in this conviction that makes him refrain from seeing Madame de Vionnet again until after the arrival of the Pococks shall free him of his responsibility as Mrs. Newsome's ambassador. When they do come, his feeling of the painful combat over Chad does not prevent his enjoyment of the comedy of Sarah's domineering rudeness and Jim's coarseness. "So do I," he tells Maria in response to her, "I revel in Sarah" (II, 135), but he is still left as the only one among the group who is not happy. "I mean they 're living. . . . I 'm waiting." And what he waits for even now is not something for himself. He continues to cling to the poor comfort of getting nothing for himself after the encounter at the Cheval Blanc has at last disclosed to him the true relation between Chad and Madame de Vionnet and after the farewell scene in her home in which all his power to see at once the shame and the appeal of her weeping and all his pity and love come out in his reflection: "She was older for him to-night, visibly less exempt from the touch of time; but she was as much as ever the finest and subtlest creature, the happiest

apparition, it had been given him, in all his years, to meet; and yet he could see her there as vulgarly troubled, in very truth, as a maidservant crying for her young man. The only thing was that she judged herself as the maid-servant would n't; the weakness of which wisdom too, the dishonour of which judgment, seemed but to sink her lower" (II, 286). Even at the end, after his hopeless effort to keep Chad faithful, it serves him as a way of refusing Maria Gostrey when he tells her he must go, "To be right. . . . That, you see, is my only logic. Not, out of the whole affair, to have got anything for myself" (II, 326). It is this fine spun logic which leads to Maria's sighing at last, "all comically, all tragically" (II, 327), as she acquiesces in his judgment.

It is right, at least, in being perfectly consistent with Strether's self-depreciating attitude in which there has always been a mixture of the tragic and the comic. There is something rueful in his assuring Maria that she will not have heard of his name. "Yet he had his reasons for not being sure but that she perhaps might" (I, 14). And later as he speaks jocosely of having his name on the green cover of the review, in answer to her, "Ah but you don't put it on for yourself," he says, "I beg your pardon—that 's exactly what I do put it on for. It 's exactly the thing that I 'm reduced to doing for myself. It seems to rescue a little, you see, from the wreck of hopes and ambitions, the refuse-heap of disappointments and failures, my one presentable little scrap of an identity" (I, 65). "He was Lambert Strether because he was on the cover, whereas it should have been, for anything like glory, that he was on the cover because he was Lambert Strether" (I, 84). He has taken obvious pleasure in calling himself to Maria "a perfectly equipped failure" (I, 44).

This self-mockery is closely linked with the feeling not only that he *has* missed his life, missed his youth, which is constantly reiterated and causes his passionate injunction to Little Bilham: "Live all you can: it 's a mistake not

to. . . . I have n't done so enough before—and now I 'm
old; too old at any rate for what I see" (I, 217), but also
that he is not *meant* to have a life of his own. In a less
often quoted part of the outburst to Little Bilham, he says
that life "could n't, no doubt, have been different for me;
for it 's at the best a tin mould, either fluted and embossed,
with ornamental excrescences, or else smooth and dreadfully
plain, into which, a helpless jelly, one's consciousness is
poured—so that one 'takes' the form, as the great cook says,
and is more or less compactly held by it: one lives in fine
as one can" (I, 218). It is his conviction that he was to
have no life of his own. "I seem to have a life only for
other people" (I, 269), he tells Miss Barrace, with a comic
enjoyment of how this fools Waymarsh, who thinks Strether
leads a very lively personal life. There is something fatalistic in his assumption that he is to be *"used"* by Chad:
"the whole thing will come upon me" (II, 140), and his
acceptance without rancor of the fact of what Madame de
Vionnet calls their thrusting on him of "appearances" (II,
287) which have made his obligation. There is nearly always some droll self-mockery in his feeling that he is to be
cheated of life, as when while he looks at the arches of
Notre Dame he thinks of Victor Hugo and wonders if
"seventy volumes in red-and-gold [were] to be perhaps
what he should most substantially have to show at Woollett
as the fruit of his mission" (II, 8). But the drollery only
emphasizes the painful sense of frustration. The acuteness
of Strether's responses increases the irony of his having no
life of his own. "It was nothing new to him . . . that a
man might have—at all events such a man as he—an amount
of experience out of any proportion to his adventures"
(I, 227). He is even capable of decisive action when it is
a question of someone else's adventures. After he has
made Chad cable Mrs. Newsome that he is not coming
home, Strether agrees with Maria's judgment that he is
wonderful. "I dare say in fact I 'm quite fantastic, and I
should n't be at all surprised if I were mad" (II, 40).

What makes Strether at once comic and tragic in his intense feeling for life and his equally strong feeling that a full experience of it is impossible for him is his awareness of his own overstrained self-consciousness. He says to Little Bilham, "I 've only my fantastic need of making my dose stiff" (II, 168), and to Maria he goes even further, "I take it too hard. . . . It makes—that 's what it comes to in the end—a fool of me" (II, 320). Strether is, indeed, made a fool of both by himself and by those whom he allows to use him. But his folly is the opposite of stupidity; and the self-awareness which creates his folly is the very source of his suffering. His understanding of his own nature and his insight into the inadequacies of each of the societies which have helped to form it clearly partake of both comic judgment and tragic vision.

There is a curious similarity in the final situation of Nanda Brookenham and Strether, both doomed to love in vain less worthy objects and to deny love to the wholly admirable and delightful Mitchy and Maria. Seeing all the weakness of Van and Madame de Vionnet, they yet utterly adore. "Ah but you 've *had* me!" (II, 289) are Strether's parting words to Maria; and having given himself to her, he can no more marry Maria, who seems a perfect companion for him, than Nanda can turn from her passion for Van, who objects to her "knowing," to marry Mitchy, who loves her the more for her very clarity of insight. The "consistency" with which they see why happiness is impossible for them is exactly what prevents their accepting any offered substitute. What seems in both of them an almost perverse refusal of happiness for themselves and for the people who love them is both comic and tragic and above all intensely human; and their superior lucidity makes all the more moving their subjection —and their subjecting others—to the common human plight.

VII ~ The Use of the Word "Funny" in the Late Novels

Disparagement of his late style has largely given place to critical appreciation of the intrinsic relation of the style to the ambiguities with which James is concerned in the novels of the "major phase."[1] Substance and form

1. As late as *The Great Tradition,* however, Leavis can speak of the "cobwebbiness that afflicted him in his late phase" [F. R. Leavis, *The Great Tradition* (New York, 1948), p. 16]. The essay deploring James's late style as a sign of "senility," (p. 126) which is reprinted in *The Great Tradition,* pp. 154-72, first appeared in *Scrutiny,* V (March, 1937), 398-417. Early objections to the change in James's style often connected it mirthfully with his beginning to dictate his work. The actual value to James of the habit of dictation in developing his "oral style" is discussed by Austin Warren, *The Rage for Order* (Chicago, 1948), p. 143. Among James's own reiterated assertions of the oneness of substance and form, a striking passage in a letter to Auguste Monod shows how strongly he held language to be a part of the essential unity. James rejoices that Monod has found *A Small Boy and Others* untranslatable: ". . . I confess that it is a relief to me this time to have so utterly defied translation. The new volume will complete that defiance and express for me how much I feel that in a literary work of the least complexity the very form and texture are the substance itself and that the flesh is indetachable from the bones! Translation is an effort—though a

are inseparable, as he repeatedly stated in his criticism and steadily demonstrated in his fiction. As he more and more abstains from narrating responses and reveals more and more directly the minds of his complicated "vessels of consciousness," the style, which is of the essence of the whole artistic unity, is bound to become more complex. James continues to show the interaction of tragedy and comedy in all the ways developed by the time of *The Portrait of a Lady;* but in addition, he increasingly depicts it in his style. The ambiguities are reflected not only in the involutions of the sentence structure, but in the very vocabulary. There is a curious stylistic imaging of the fusion of tragedy and comedy in his use of the word "funny" in the late novels. As he uses it in progressively more sinister circumstances, he seems to add tragic overtones to the meanings of "queer" and "ironic"; yet the very homeliness of the word makes it retain the element of laughter.

In *The Ambassadors,* the fact that the word sometimes has, at least for the user of it, no more than the ordinary sense of "amusing" calls special attention to its sometimes carrying more meaning—as it regularly does for Strether. When Miss Barrace says of Waymarsh, "He 's too funny" (*The Ambassadors,* I, 206), she means simply that he is "amusing," a word which she uses in the same sentence to describe his imperviousness to any impression of Europe. "I show him Paris, show him everything, and he never turns a hair. He 's like the Indian chief one reads about, who, when he comes up to Washington to see the Great Father, stands wrapt in his blanket and gives no sign" (I, 206). For Miss Barrace, with her highly developed sense of comedy, this is pure entertainment. "He does n't understand—not one little scrap. He 's delightful. He 's wonderful" (I, 205). Waymarsh is funny in this sense for

---

most flattering one!—to *tear* the hapless flesh, and in fact to get rid of so much of it that the living thing bleeds and faints away! forgive the violence of my figure" [*The Selected Letters of Henry James,* ed. Leon Edel (New York, 1955), p. 107].

the reader too since James's treatment of him is steadily
and gaily satiric. But because the citizen of Milrose is an
embodiment of the whole set of attitudes represented for
Strether by Woollett, Waymarsh's rigidity cannot be for
him simply laughable. Miss Barrace's sally of imagination
is met "with frank amusement on Bilham's part and a
shade of sadness on Strether's. Strether's sadness sprang—
for the image had its grandeur—from his thinking how
little he himself was wrapt in his blanket, how little, in
marble halls, all too oblivious of the Great Father, he resembled a really majestic aboriginal" (I, 206). Yet his
sharing some of Waymarsh's preconceptions is emphasized
by his immediately raising the question of whether his
Parisian friends have not substituted the visual sense for
the moral and wondering if in the light of Paris things can
show for what they really are, to get from Little Bilham the
teasing reply,

"Oh I like your Boston 'reallys' ! But sometimes—
yes."

"Dear old Paris then!" Strether resignedly sighed
while for a moment they looked at each other. Then he
broke out: "Does Madame de Vionnet do that? I mean
really show for what she is?" (I, 207-8).
When Miss Barrace suggests putting the question to the
lady herself,

"No," said Little Bilham; "don't put any question;
wait, rather—it will be much more fun—to judge for yourself."

Fun, Strether does have—fun "enough to last me
for the rest of my days" (II, 35) he tells Chad; but his
response has given the word such a weight of meaning that
"Chad looked amused and interested, yet still somewhat in
the dark; partly perhaps because Strether's estimate of
fun had required of him from the first a good deal of eluci-
dation." The conversation with Chad is the result of
Strether's decision to refuse Mrs. Newsome's summons to

him to come home, because of his certitude "that has
passed through the fire." He challenges Chad:

". . . Stay on with me. . . ."

". . . But what, my dear man," Chad went on with
conscious queerness, "does it all lead to for you?"

The change of position and of relation, for each,
was so oddly betrayed in the question that Chad laughed
out as soon as he had uttered it—which made Strether also
laugh. (II, 34-35).

The use of the word "fun" follows this exchange, and the
context gives it, when it comes, the power to suggest all
the serious implications of Strether's change of sides in the
contest for Chad.

Chad himself is as "easy" in his acquiescence as he
is about everything. "He was easy, always, when he understood; he was easier still, if possible, when he did n't" (I,
258-59). His "easiness" is shown in his attitude to Strether's
scruples. When Strether has refused to dine with Madame
de Vionnet, Chad has substituted a party at his own "lovely home." He had "replied that he would make it all right;
and he had proceeded to do this by substituting the present
occasion—as he was ready to substitute others—for any,
for every occasion as to which his old friend should have
a funny scruple" (I, 259). For Chad, Strether's scruples
remain funny simply in the sense of being odd and amusing; but for Strether, who sees them partly as they appear
to Chad, they are also a highly serious element of his perplexity. As he waits for the descent of the Pococks and
reflects on Waymarsh's part in bringing them to Paris,
he comes back to what he does and does not have in
common with the "pilgrim from Milrose."

> Waymarsh . . . confessed to nothing; and though
> this falsified in some degree Strether's forecast the
> latter amusedly saw in it the same depth of good
> conscience out of which the dear man's impertinence
> had originally sprung. He was patient with the dear
> man now and delighted to observe how unmistak-

ably he had put on flesh; he felt his own holiday so
successfully large and free that he was full of allowances and charities in respect to those cabined and
confined: his instinct toward a spirit so strapped
down as Waymarsh's was to walk round it on tiptoe
for fear of waking it up to a sense of losses by this
time irretrievable. It was all very funny, he knew,
and but the difference, as he often said to himself,
of tweedledum and tweedledee—an emancipation so
purely comparative that it was like the advance of
the door-mat on the scraper; yet the present crisis
was happily to profit by it and the pligrim from
Milrose to know himself more than ever in the right
(II, 57).

Strether's ability to make this kind of humorous comparison between himself and Waymarsh, to see it as "all
very funny," is what chiefly complicates, indeed creates,
his whole predicament.

The word "fun" is exchanged between Strether and
Maria as they discuss the advent of the Pococks and gathers
ambiguity in the course of the conversation. Maria has
declared that Strether's staying to see what will happen
will be "immense fun" (II, 42). Then James builds up
through the following interchange the accretions which
the word carries when Strether echoes it:

". . . and to see you work it out will be one of the
sensations of my life. It *is* clear you can toddle
alone!"

He received this tribute without elation. "I
shan't be alone when the Pococks have come."

Her eyebrows went up. "The Pococks are
coming?"

"That, I mean, is what will happen—and
happen as quickly as possible—in consequence of
Chad's cable. They 'll simply embark. Sarah will
come to speak for her mother—with an effect different from *my* muddle."

Miss Gostrey more gravely wondered. "*She*
then will take him back?"

"Very possibly—and we shall see. She must at

any rate have the chance, and she may be trusted to do all she can."

"And do you *want* that?"

"Of course," said Strether, "I want it. I want to play fair."

But she had lost for a moment the thread. "If it devolves on the Pococks why do you stay?"

"Just to see that I *do* play fair—and a little also, no doubt, that they do." Strether was luminous as he had never been. "I came out to find myself in presence of new facts—facts that have kept striking me as less and less met by our old reasons. The matter's perfectly simple. New reasons—reasons as new as the facts themselves—are wanted; and of this our friends at Woollett—Chad's and mine—were at the earliest moment definitely notified. If any are producible Mrs. Pocock will produce them; she 'll bring over the whole collection. They 'll be," he added with a pensive smile, "a part of the 'fun' you speak of" (II, 42-44).

The word "funny" recurs throughout the visit of the Pococks, whom James gleefully satirizes and at the same time shows as bringing disaster to Strether. When Strether, in the cab on the way to the hotel, has to submit to Jim Pocock's vulgar insinuations about the good time he and Chad are having in Paris, "a play of innuendo as vague as a nursery-rhyme, yet as aggressive as an elbow in his side," he gradually realizes that Jim sees nothing of the transformation in Chad. "It was what he had taken his own stand on, so far as he had taken a stand; and if they were all only going to see nothing he had only wasted his time. He gave his friend till the very last moment, till they had come into sight of the hotel; and when poor Pocock only continued cheerful and envious and funny he fairly grew to dislike him, to feel him extravagantly common" (II, 88). Part of what the word carries here is the simple meaning which Pocock attaches to it with his cheap jokes about the life to be led in Paris; but it also seems to Strether funny in the sense of queer that Jim can

be so blind. And as the drive ends, Strether is feeling not only the queerness, but the direness, of the Woollett attitude. Jim says with school boy delight in his own facetiousness that Mrs. Newsome is sitting up " 'All night, my boy—for *you*!' And Jim fetched him, with a vulgar little guffaw, a thrust that gave relief to the picture. But he had got what he wanted. He felt on the spot that this *was* the real word from Woollett. 'So don't you go home!' Jim added while he alighted and while his friend, letting him profusely pay the cabman, sat on in a momentary muse. Strether wondered if that were the real word too" (II, 89).

All of the group come within the orbit of the funny. Maria "funnily" considers the comedy of Waymarsh's assiduous attentions to Sarah. Strether says he is "floating her over, by kindness," and Maria caps the phrase, "floating her over in champagne?" (II, 136, 137). Madame de Vionnet is funny in her courage when she sets about captivating Jim Pocock in her desperate hope of winning over Chad's family.

. . . "It must be funny."

"Oh it *is* funny." That of course essentially went with it.

But it brought them back. "How indeed she must care!" (II, 182). Even Mamie has her funny aspect. "Yes, she was funny, wonderful Mamie, and without dreaming it; she was bland, she was bridal—with never, that he could make out as yet, a bridegroom to support it; she was handsome and portly and easy and chatty, soft and sweet and almost disconcertingly reassuring" (II, 149). Then James —or Strether—gives the physical description which sounds wholly satiric until he pulls up with: "But if all this was where she was funny, and if what was funnier than the rest was the contrast between her beautiful benevolent patronage—such a hint of the polysyllabic as might make her something of a bore toward middle age—and her rather flat little voice, the voice, naturally, unaffectedly yet, of a girl of fifteen; so Strether, none the less, at the end of

ten minutes, felt in her a quiet dignity that pulled things bravely together" (II, 150). Mamie has been brought out to detach Chad from his Paris entanglement by marrying him; but Strether perceives that she is "of all people, as might have been said, on the side and of the party of Mrs. Newsome's original ambassador. . . . It fully came up for them then, by means of their talking of everything *but* Chad, that Mamie, unlike Sarah, unlike Jim, knew perfectly what had become of him. It fully came up that she had taken to the last fraction of an inch the measure of the change in him, and that she wanted Strether to know what a secret she proposed to make of it" (II, 150-51).

The word introduces the final confrontation between Strether and Sarah Pocock. When Waymarsh announced her visit, Strether "saw on the spot what had happened, and what probably would yet; and it was all funny enough. It was perhaps just this freedom of appreciation that wound him up to his flare of high spirits. 'What is she coming *for?*—to kill me?'" (II, 188). Waymarsh, humorless as always, assures him that Sarah is coming to be kind; and Strether, who feels the straight line of communication from Woollett in this answer, teases Waymarsh into the awkward necessity of lying about what he knows of Woollett affairs. Strether "enjoyed for the moment—as for the first time in his life—the sense of so carrying it off. He wondered—it was amusing—if he felt as the impudent feel" (II, 189). His enjoyment of Waymarsh's discomfiture is real; but so is his awareness that Sarah *is* coming in effect to "kill" him.

When Sarah does come, Strether greets her by praising the good she has done to Waymarsh. "It was a plunge because somehow the range of reference was, in the conditions, 'funny,' and made funnier still by Sarah's attitude, by the turn the occasion had, with her appearance, so sensibly taken. Her appearance was really indeed funnier than anything else—the spirit in which he felt her to be

there as soon as she *was* there, the shade of obscurity that cleared up for him as soon as he was seated with her in the small *salon de lecture*. . . . She had come to receive his submission, and Waymarsh was to have made it plain to him that she would expect nothing less. He saw fifty things, her host, at this convenient stage; but one of those he most saw was that their anxious friend had n't quite had the hand required of him" (II, 195, 196-97). As she comes to the point and her accusations grow sharper and sharper, Strether reaches the conclusion: "She was n't at all funny at last—she was really fine; and he felt easily where she was strong—strong for herself. It had n't yet so come home to him that she was nobly and appointedly officious. She was acting in interests grander and clearer than that of her poor little personal, poor little Parisian equilibrium, and all his consciousness of her mother's moral pressure profited by this proof of its sustaining force" (II, 198). As she speaks in righteous indignation, heaping insults upon Strether, upon Madame de Vionnet, and upon the effect of his life in Paris on Chad, which she calls "hideous" (II, 205), she sinks into the kind of straightforward abuse which is merely painful. The doubleness of attitude which has enabled Strether to find her approach funny is no longer possible. "She had let fly at him as from a stretched cord, and it took him a minute to recover from the sense of being pierced" (II, 205-6). Early in the novel upon Chad's return to Paris Strether has felt the necessity of preventing any levity in Chad's reports to Mrs. Newsome of her ambassador's relation with Maria Gostrey. "It was accordingly to forestall such an accident that he frankly put before the young man the several facts, just as they had occurred, of his funny alliance. He spoke of these facts, pleasantly and obligingly, as 'the whole story,' and felt that he might qualify the alliance as funny if he remained sufficiently grave about it" (I, 162-63). This early use of the word gives some suggestion of the range of implication it has in the novel and its connection with the im-

portance of the right social nuance. But Sarah in her open display of wrath and reprobation has moved out of the orbit of the funny and the grave alike, out of the state in which any kind of social attitude is possible. Her exhibition of bad manners at least makes clear her position that "all 's at an end." Strether is left facing the fact that "it probably *was* all at an end" (II, 205, 206).

But he has still to encounter his disillusionment about the relation between Chad and Madame de Vionnet —which makes him judge differently all that Madame de Vionnet has represented for him—and the evidence of Chad's faithlessness. Toward the end of his day in the country he sees a "boat advancing round the bend and containing a man who held the paddles and a lady, at the stern, with a pink parasol," and feels that it is "exactly the right thing" (II, 256) for the Lambinet picture, the image of which has dominated the day for him. The irony of his pleasure is increased by the reflections which have preceded it: "That was part of the amusement—as if to show that the fun was harmless" (II, 254). Almost as soon as the identity of the pair is clear to him, it is equally clear that the fun is not harmless; but all three conspire, the men taking their cue from Madame de Vionnet, to keep up the pretense that it is. "It had been a performance, Madame de Vionnet's manner" (II, 263), of acting as if their presence were simply a matter of a day in the country like his own. "Her shawl and Chad's overcoat and her other garments, and his, those they had each worn the day before, were at the place, best known to themselves— a quiet retreat enough, no doubt—at which they had been spending the twenty-four hours, to which they had fully meant to return that evening, from which they had so remarkably swum into Strether's ken, and the tacit repudiation of which had been thus the essence of her comedy" (II, 264-65). In this comedy is implicit all the tragedy made explicit in the parting scene between Strether and Madame de Vionnet, which shortly follows it. "Away from them,

during his vigil, he had seemed to wince at the amount of comedy involved; whereas in his present posture he could only ask himself how he should enjoy any attempt from her to take the comedy back. He should n't enjoy it at all; but, once more and yet once more, he could trust her. That is he could trust her to make deception right. As she presented things the ugliness—goodness knew why— went out of them; none the less too that she could present them, with an art of her own, by not so much as touching them" (II, 277). She does not need to touch the comedy of her yesterday's deception, which she perfectly knows has not deceived Strether. What she does now touch directly for the first time is her tragedy: her fear of desertion by Chad. In the whole kaleidoscope of appearance and reality which has moved before Strether's vision, the comedy has turned up tragedy.[2]

All that remains of Strether's "fun" after that farewell is to try to make Chad see that he will be the cad his name suggests if he deserts Madame de Vionnet. He does speak in the strongest terms, only to draw from Chad the callow declaration: "I give you my word of honour . . . that I 'm not a bit tired of her" (II, 312). Strether is stunned into silence by the complacent heartlessness of tone, even though he knows of Chad's fickleness. He has discovered in talking to Madame de Vionnet that she knows that Chad is already tired of her and yet she clings to him: "she had but made Chad what he was—so why could she think she had made him infinite? She had made him better, she had made him best, she had made him anything one would; but it came to our friend with su-

2. Maurice Bewley uses the image of a trap door opening on tragedy; but as his phrase "shifting distinction" shows, even the "subterranean regions" are not unambiguously tragic: "The shifting distinction between comedy and tragedy is, perhaps, finally dependent on a radical ambiguity in the nature of moral experience itself, but whatever the explanation, the comic effects that James brings off on his carefully plotted stage frequently seem to be performed on trap doors opening immediately into subterranean regions of a vastly different character" [*The Complex Fate* (London, 1952), pp. 16-17].

preme queerness that he was none the less only Chad" (II, 284). His being still *"our* little Chad" (II, 301) brings back with ironic force Strether's early musings over Chad's transformation "as he funnily fancied it" (I, 153). His imagination "had faced every contingency but that Chad should not *be* Chad, and this was what it now had to face" (I, 136-37).

At Chad's party for Sarah, Miss Barrace with her usual boldness of candor has told Strether that she knows what it's a question of:

"Oh everyone must know now," poor Strether thoughtfully admitted; "and it 's strange enough and funny enough that one should feel everybody here at this very moment to be knowing and watching and waiting."

"Yes—is n't it indeed funny?" Miss Barrace quite rose to it, "That 's the way we *are* in Paris." She was always pleased with a new contribution to that queerness (II, 179).

Though the word is not used again in the conversation, the rest of it is full of the painful funniness of Strether's position as hero of the contest over Chad and his uneasiness before the difficulties of such a position. As reluctant a hero as he is, he engages his antagonists one after another, until he confronts the tragedy of defeat. But even his sense of defeat is still complicated by his awareness of comic irony. As Maria tells him of Madame de Vionnet's anxiety in her ignorance of Chad's whereabouts, "he had one of the last flickers of his occasional mild mirth. 'To think that was just what I came out to prevent!' " (II, 298). Even in his final visit to Maria when he reports his remonstrating with Chad and Chad's callousness toward Madame de Vionnet, he retains a sense of comic incongruity as well as of more suffering to come from Chad's inconstancy. "I 've done . . . what I could—one can 't do more. He protests his devotion and his horror. But I 'm not sure I 've saved him. He protests too much. He asks how one can dream of his being tired. But he has all life before him" (II,

324-25). And so the novel moves through Strether's refusal
of the solace Maria offers him to its "funny" conclusion:
" 'Then there we are!' said Strether" (II, 327).

~   ~   ~

In *The Wings of the Dove* again the word "funny"
is likely to suggest the extremely unfunny. It is first used
in the opening scene to describe the effect upon Kate of
the entrance of her father, whose "perfect look, which had
floated him so long, was practically perfect still" (*The
Wings of the Dove*, I, 8). As she has waited for him, his
daughter has reflected that "he dealt out lies as he might
the cards from the greasy old pack for the game of di-
plomacy to which you were to sit down with him. . . . he
breathed upon the tragic consciousness in such a way that
after a moment nothing of it was left. The difficulty was
not less that he breathed in the same way upon the comic:
she almost believed that with this latter she might still
have found a foothold for clinging to him. He had ceased
to be amusing—he was really too inhuman" (I, 7-8). So
when he finally enters after making the girl he has sum-
moned wait an unconscionable time, "the one stray gleam
of comedy . . . in his daughter's eyes was the funny feeling
he momentarily made her have of being herself 'looked up'
by him in sordid lodgings. For a minute after he came in
it was as if the place were her own and he the visitor with
susceptibilities. He gave you funny feelings, he had in-
describable arts, that quite turned the tables."[3] With this
introduction, James proceeds to give the scene a kind of
dreadful comedy as he presents the discomfiture of Lionel

3. The text reproducing the original version of 1902 from which
this passage is quoted is the Century Library Edition (London,
1948), p. 14. In the New York Edition James changed both of these
uses of "funny" to "absurd" (I, 8). The more extreme word intensifies the sinister incongruity, but the earlier choice of "funny" keeps
more of the possibility of laughter in the grim comedy.

Croy at Kate's urging him to let her live with him. "He wished her not to come to him, still less to settle with him, and had sent for her to give her up with some style and state; a part of the beauty of which, however, was to have been his sacrifice to her own detachment. There was no style, no state, unless she wished to forsake him. His idea had accordingly been to surrender her to her wish with all nobleness; it had by no means been to have positively to keep her off" (I, 10). But the satiric exposure of the selfishness of the debased schemer is darkened throughout by the despair of Kate, whose sense of physical sickness at one point images the sickening effect of the whole scene. Long before her father has reached the end of his brazen proposals for "working" Aunt Maud, Kate has risen "as if in sight of the term of her effort, in sight of the futility and the weariness of many things, and moved back to the poor little glass" to adjust her hat. The sight of her before the mirror "brought to her father's lips another remark— in which impatience . . . had already been replaced by a funny flare of appreciation. 'Oh, you're all right! Don't muddle yourself up with *me!* '"[4] Whatever is funny in Lionel Croy is sinister; and the feeling evoked by the comedy of his self-revelation is horror. The corresponding pity for Kate and admiration for her strength and courage, thus firmly established in the prominence of the opening scene, are never wholly lost even in the greater pity for Milly as her victim.

The novel contains other simpler uses of the word "funny," simple at least from the point of view of those in whose stream of consciousness they occur. When Milly sends off Susan Stringham with Mrs. Lowder to go to the party from which Milly herself is staying at home with Kate, Aunt Maud accepts the situation with her usual complacency about her own good nature. The consistent arrogance of her condescension toward Mrs. Stringham is

4. Century Library Edition, p. 18. In the New York Edition James changes "funny" to the ironic "free" (I, 16).

in her use of the word funny. "If it was n't quite Aunt
Maud's ideal, . . . to take out the new American girl's
funny friend instead of the new American girl herself,
nothing could better indicate the range of that lady's merit
than the spirit in which—as at the present hour for instance
—she made the best of the minor advantage. And she did
this with a broad cheerful absence of illusion; she did it—
confessing even as much to poor Susie—because, frankly,
she *was* good-natured. When Mrs. Stringham observed that
her own light was too abjectly borrowed and that it was
as a link alone, fortunately not missing, that she was valued,
Aunt Maud concurred to the extent of the remark: 'Well,
my dear, you 're better than nothing' " (I, 263). It is
while Susie has left them to get ready to go out that Aunt
Maud broaches with Milly the subject of Densher, and
Milly reflects that she cannot "judge from her face of her
uppermost motive—it was so little, in its hard smooth sheen,
that kind of human countenance. She looked hard when
she spoke fair; the only thing was that when she spoke hard
she did n't likewise look soft" (I, 269). The hardness
behind the metallic face James has underlined by letting
Aunt Maud think of Susie merely as "the new American
girl's funny friend" and then calculate the value of the
"funny friend" as a "minor advantage."

The word "funny" is differently connected with
Aunt Maud in Densher's stream of consciousness. When
he is exposed to the "prodigious extent" of her "vast draw-
ing-room," he thinks of her first as simply "colossally
vulgar" (I, 76, 77). But her surroundings suggest something much more sinister than vulgarity.

> It was the language of the house itself that spoke
> to him, writing out for him, with surpassing breadth
> and freedom the associations and conceptions, the
> ideals and possibilities of the mistress. Never, he
> felt sure, had he seen so many things so unanimous-
> ly ugly—operatively, ominously so cruel. He was
> glad to have found this last name for the whole

character; "cruel" somehow played into the subject for an article—an article that his impression put straight into his mind. He would write about the heavy horrors that could still flourish, that lifted their undiminished heads, in an age so proud of its short way with false gods; and it would be funny if what he should have got from Mrs. Lowder were to prove after all but a small amount of copy. Yet the great thing, really the dark thing, was that, even while he thought of the quick column he might add up, he felt it less easy to laugh at the heavy horrors than to quail before them (I, 78).

Mrs. Lowder's own use of the word "funny" to characterize Susie is a perfectly straightforward rendering of a fixed attitude; the complicating overtones come from outside her consciousness. Here, however, in a much more subtle mind, James shows the sense of the term changing from simple to complex in Densher's own awareness. It occurs to him merely in the meaning of queer: it would be queer if such lavish material did not provide a large quantity of copy. But it gets connected as he uses it with the satiric viewpoint from which the article would be written. His judgment has already moved from "ugly" to "cruel"; and as the word "funny" suggests laughter to him, he realizes that the "heavy horrors" hold a power which is beyond satiric laughter. Nevertheless, when Mrs. Lowder appears, Densher finds her "bland" and perceives that the game is to be more complicated than her display of power has suggested. He finds the prospect amusing in the Jamesian sense of that word. "There would never be mistakes but for the original fun of mistakes" (I, 80).

The most pervasive use of the word "funny" is in Milly's attitudes. Her response to Susie's use of the word "fun" in somewhat the same meaning as Densher's "original fun of mistakes," to suggest the risk of renewing acquaintance with her girlhood friend Maud Manningham, is: "Risk everything!" (I, 140). And after she is launched in London society, she turns Susie's word back on her:

Susie had an intense thought and then an effusion. "My dear child, we move in a labyrinth."

"Of course we do. That 's just the fun of it!" said Milly with a strange gaiety. Then she added: "Don't tell me that—in this for instance—there are not abysses. I want abysses" (I, 186).

What they are discussing at the moment is Aunt Maud's fear of an attachment between Kate and Densher which will stand in the way of her plan to marry Kate to Lord Mark. But what has come out just before is that Milly has heard "never a word" (I, 185) from Kate on the subject of Densher, and she is led to revise her view of the last days of intimate talk with Kate: "it now came over her as in a clear cold wave that there was a possible account of their relations in which the quantity her new friend had told her might have figured as small, as smallest, beside the quantity she had n't. . . . Somehow, for Milly, brush it over nervously as she might and with whatever simplifying hand, this abrupt extrusion of Mr. Densher altered all proportions, had an effect on all values" (I, 187-88). She chides herself as fantastic to let it make a difference and even to think of Densher's silence in New York as an "abyss." So she does her best to hide the fact that it does make a difference and chatters to Susie about the oddity of their all knowing Mr. Densher: "it was amusing—oh awfully amusing!—to be able fondly to hope that there was 'something *in*' its having been left to crop up with such suddenness" (I, 188-89). When Milly sees Kate again and finds her still silent, "her silence succeeded in passing muster with her as the beginning of a new sort of fun. The sort was all the newer by its containing measurably a small element of anxiety: when she had gone in for fun before it had been with her hands a little more free" (I, 189). The funniness of such new fun she further experiences when she comes on Kate and Densher, who have been having a morning alone at the National Gallery. "It took, no doubt, a big dose of inspiration to treat as not funny

—or at least as not unpleasant—the anomaly, for Kate, that *she* knew their gentleman, and for herself, that Kate was spending the morning with him" (I, 295).

By the word "funny" Milly regularly means "queer" as well as "laughable"; and as applied to herself it is a recurrent part of her attempt to manage what is painful. In the scene in which she recognizes her resemblance to the Bronzino portrait: "a very great personage—only un-accompanied by a joy. And she was dead, dead, dead" (I, 221), it is through tears that she laughs, "Of course her complexion 's green, . . . but mine 's several shades greener. . . . Her hands are large, . . . but mine are larger. Mine are huge." Finally she calls the notion of the resemblance a "funny fancy" (I, 222).

Poignant as this conversation is, it is not more so than the entirely interior monologue in the Regent's Park after Milly has learned from Sir Luke that she is indeed gravely ill. She feels that she has in a manner caught him "in a cleft stick: she either mattered, and then she was ill; or she did n't matter, and then she was well enough. . . . He *had* distinguished her—that was the chill. He had n't known—how could he?—that she was devilishly subtle, subtle in exactly the manner of the suspected, the suspicious, the condemned. He in fact confessed to it, in his way, as to an interest in her combinations, her funny race, her funny losses, her funny gains, her funny freedom, and, no doubt, above all her funny manners—funny, like those of Amer-icans at their best, without being vulgar, legitimating ami-ability and helping to pass it off" (I, 253).

There is an echo of this view of Milly's funniness as a source of interest and kindness in Densher's comment at the dinner party in Lancaster Gate, from which Milly has stayed away. Mrs. Lowder, who has persistently made her the subject of conversation, finally asks Densher "if it were true that their friend had really not made in her own country the mark she had chalked so large in London" (II, 39). In answer, he suggests that: "it would n't be the

first time, . . . that they had taught the Americans to appreciate (especially when it was funny) some native product. He did n't mean that Miss Theale was funny—though she was weird, and this was precisely her magic." Mrs. Stringham's "feverish sally," in which she shows the superior taste of Boston in appreciating Milly and makes "her nearest approach to supplying the weirdness in which Milly's absence had left them deficient," ends with her addressing to Densher the sharp rebuke: "You know nothing, sir—but not the least little bit—about my friend" (II, 40). He tries to mollify her by saying that he knows only how kind Milly has been to him in New York and how much he has appreciated it; and before long the comedy of the little exchange has ended in looks of friendly communication between Densher and Susie. But Densher's proclaiming the very view of Milly which she has attributed to Sir Luke adds to the irony of her being in love with Densher and her then being "successfully deceived" (II, 69) by Aunt Maud's lie, transmitted through Susie, that Kate does not care for him.

"What might really *become* in all this of the American girl" (II, 66) is a question that troubles Densher, though he has conceded that Kate's "queer" plan is "amusing" (II, 64). Aunt Maud, with purposes opposite from Kate's, also tries to bribe him with Milly's fortune: "The pieces fell together for him as he felt her thus buying him off, and buying him—it would have been funny if it had n't been so grave—with Miss Theale's money" (II, 67).

As the net of their designs begins to tighten around Milly, Kate's bold warning to her recurs with redoubled force to the reader, but not to Milly herself. In the last conversation between the two girls before Densher's return from America initiates a new movement of the drama, Kate has spoken with astonishing frankness of the threat to Milly in the whole mercenary scheme of values in the world of Lancaster Gate. "We 're of no use to you—it 's decent to tell you. You 'd be of use to us, but that 's a

different matter. My honest advice to you would be . . .
to drop us while you can. It would be funny if you did n't
soon see how awfully better you can do" (I, 281). Though
she is speaking honestly, Kate is herself the chief threat,
as Milly perceives in her image of Kate as a pacing panther.
"That was a violent image, but it made her a little less
ashamed of having been scared" (I, 282). But she is not
scared enough to heed the funniness Kate has spoken of;
and so with conscious deliberation she takes up her rôle
as dove.

Perhaps the most ironic use of the word in the whole
novel occurs in Densher's rueful pondering over the changed
relation between himself and Kate after his return from
Venice: "He would have described their change—had he
so far faced it as to describe it—by their being so damned
civil. That had even, with the intimate, the familiar at
the point to which they had brought them, a touch almost
of the funny. What danger had there ever been of their
becoming rude—after each had, long since, made the other
so tremendously tender? Such were the things he asked
himself when he wondered what in particular he most
feared."[5] What he has to fear becomes steadily clearer.
Milly's wings stretch even to cover them, as Kate and Densher tell each other at the end; but they must perforce be
covered in different ways: Kate, presumably, by the money
and Densher by the memory of Milly. Their relation not
only with each other, but with the dead Milly, has grown
too "funny" to be simply resolved. All the reverberations
of the word are behind Kate's final line: "We shall never
be again as we were" (II, 405).

~   ~   ~

In *The Golden Bowl* the word "funny" takes on its
most sinister overtones because it is linked with what Mag-

5. Century Library Edition, p. 407. In the New York Edition
James changed the word "funny" to "droll" (II, 393-94), which
operates even more strongly.

gie calls "the queer things in our life" (*The Golden Bowl,*
II, 113). But it is first used to define the differences among
the characters out of which the strange situation grows. A
use which begins early in the novel and continues throughout is that of label for what one character finds odd, and
often appealing, in another. The Prince is talking about
the Ververs as being romantic without folly when he tells
Maggie before he marries her: "Only the funny thing . . .
was that her father, though older and wiser, and a man
into the bargain, was as bad—that is as good—as herself"
(I, 11). Much later Fanny Assingham applies the term
directly to Mr. Verver in expressing her bewilderment
about him. She calls him, "Charlotte's too inconceivably
funny husband" (II, 135), and Colonel Assingham accuses
her of never speaking of him but "*as* too inconceivably
funny."

"Well, he is," she always confessed. "That is he may
be, for all I know, too inconceivably great. But that 's not
an idea. It represents only my weak necessity of feeling
that he 's beyond me—which is n't an idea either. You
see he may be stupid too."

"Precisely—there you are."

"Yet on the other hand," she always went on, "he
may be sublime: sublimer even than Maggie herself. He
may in fact have already been. But we shall never know"
(II, 135).
Fanny's alternatives remain live possibilities in judging
the "little man" who is perhaps the most ambiguous of the
characters.

Mr. Verver is strange to the Prince not only in his
romanticism, but also in his morality. Amerigo is being
deliberately funny for Mrs. Assingham's diversion in the
terms he uses to contrast the Anglo-Saxon and the Roman
moral sense; but under the wit he shows very clearly that
he sees possible difficulty in the difference between the
"tortuous stone staircase" of his conscience and Mr. Verver's " 'lightning elevator' . . . he developed, making her

laugh, his idea that the tea of the English race was somehow their morality, 'made,' with boiling water, in a little
pot, so that the more of it one drank the more moral one
would become. . . . He was funny, while they talked,
about his own people too, whom he described, with anec-
dotes of their habits, imitations of their manners and
prophecies of their conduct, as more *rococo* than anything
Cadogan Place would ever have known" (I, 31, 32).

The Prince, of course, is correspondingly funny in
the eyes of the Anglo-Saxons, even those of the Europeanized Charlotte, who feels indulgent toward "his funny
Italian taste for London street-life" (I, 114) and even
toward his Italian way of saying that his sense of omens
will protect him. "It was funny, the way he said such
things; yet she liked him, really, the more for it."[6] Charlotte has defined the word in speaking of the gift she wants
to find as a wedding present for Maggie:

He recalled even how he had been struck with her
word. " 'Funny'?"

"Oh, I don't mean a comic toy—I mean some little
thing with a charm. But absolutely *right,* in its comparative cheapness. That 's what I call funny" (I, 92).

The Prince's funny Italian ways clearly have for Charlotte
the charm of being "absolutely *right.*" For Maggie too the
term includes loving appreciation when she thinks of his
"funny Italian anxiety" (I, 160), which she hopes Fanny
will take care of if the Prince notices her going off with
her father for the first of the long conversations at Fawns.

The charm of the Prince's funny foreignness operates not only on the women in the novel. Mr. Verver also
rejoices in his "roundness." But there is something almost
perverse in his finding amusement in perplexing Amerigo
by his adoration of his grandson. Amerigo's "discriminations in respect to his heir were in fine not more angular

6. Quoted from the Laurel Edition, which reproduces the original text (New York, 1963), p. 93. In the New York Edition James
changes Charlotte's second use of the word to "droll" (I, 120).

than any others to be observed in him; and Mr. Verver
received perhaps from no source so distinct an impression
of being for him an odd and important phenomenon as
he received from this impunity of appropriation, these
unchallenged nursery hours. . . . Little by little thus from
month to month the Prince was learning what his wife's
father had been brought up to; and now it could be checked
off—he had been brought up to the romantic view of
principini. . . . The only fear somewhat sharp for Mr.
Verver was a certain fear of disappointing him for strangeness. . . . He did n't know—he was learning, and it was
funny for him—to how many things he *had* been brought
up. If the Prince could only strike something to which
he had n't! This would n't, it seemed to him, ruffle the
smoothness and yet *might* a little add to the interest" (I,
157-58).

The characters in *The Golden Bowl* not only find
each other funny; they also use the word to judge other
impressions. When Charlotte goes with Mr. Verver to the
house of Mr. Gutermann-Seuss, she "noticed everything, as
from the habit of a person finding her account at any time,
according to a wisdom well learned of life, in almost any
'funny' impression. It really came home to her friend
on the spot that this free range of observation in her, picking out the frequent funny with extraordinary promptness,
would verily henceforth make a different thing for him of
such experiences, of the customary hunt for the possible
prize, the inquisitive play of his accepted monomania"
(I, 213). Mr. Verver's noticing Charlotte's noticing gives
a kind of Chinese box effect to the layers of connoisseurship. Charlotte collects funny impressions as Mr. Verver
collects art treasures and is now collecting Charlotte with
the ironic idea that she will add to his own fun.

Maggie too uses the word to describe impressions.
Sometimes she uses it in Charlotte's sense; in fact, she is
quoting Charlotte to herself when she remembers the
allusion to "funny little fascinating" (II, 155) places in

Bloomsbury, shops where treasures may still be picked up. There is only pleasure in her thinking of the "fun" of giving presents to her father, who cherishes them for their friendliness almost in proportion as they are "foredoomed aberration[s]" (II, 156) for him as a collector. "She was now ready to try it again: they had always, with his plea-sure in her pretense and her pleasure in his, with the funny betrayal of the sacrifice to domestic manners on either side, played the game so happily" (II, 157). There is nothing in Maggie's consciousness to complicate the affectionate appreciation of her father's oddity in pretend-ing that her birthday gifts are the prizes of his collection. But the reference to Charlotte and to the little shops in Bloomsbury make the word carry ironic overtones of which Maggie herself is unaware.

Maggie, however, frequently calls things funny with much more complex intention. Her use of the word in connection with Mrs. Rance is one of the ways of empha-sizing the parallel, one of the central patterns in the formal design of the novel, of the long conversations with her father at Fawns. When she first talks to him to suggest marriage as a way of saving him from pursuit, Mr. Verver has acknowledged that he finds Mrs. Rance formidable:

"Oh well, I 'd help you," the Princess said with decision, "as against *her*—if that 's all you require. It 's too funny," she went on before he again spoke, "that Mrs. Rance should be here at all. But if you talk of the life we lead much of it 's altogether, I 'm bound to say, too funny. The thing is," Maggie developed under this impression, "that I don't think we lead, as regards other people, any life at all" (I, 175).

And thus she launches her idea of their becoming "grander" by bringing in Charlotte "because she 's so great" (I, 180). Maggie's echo of her own word "funny" moves the conversation into a new level and precipitates what might be called the "argument" both of the interview and of the action of the novel. When the word is used to intro-

duce the parallel conversation in Book V where Adam
realizes that he must remove the still "great" Charlotte,
it carries not only all the weight of Maggie's intervening
anguish, but also an immediate ironic reminder of the
earlier crucial conversation between father and daughter,
and Maggie's early references to Charlotte's greatness; to
the Prince's magnificence: "He *could* be a hero—he *will*
be one if it 's ever necessary. But it will be about something better than our dreariness. *I* know . . . where he 's
magnificent"; and to her own living in terror: "I do always
by nature, tremble for my life" (I, 176, 181). The second
long conversation is placed three days in time, but immediately in the sequence of the novel, after the scene on
the terrace with Charlotte has shown Maggie at the crisis
when she most trembles for her life. Adam's question
about how Maggie now regards "the once formidable Mrs.
Rance" is what makes the father and daughter feel the
need to talk as they had "on the occasion of the previous
visit of these anciently more agitating friends—that of
their long talk on a sequestered bench beneath one of the
great trees, when the particular question had come up
for them the then purblind discussion of which at their
enjoyed leisure Maggie had formed the habit of regarding as the 'first beginning' of their present situation. . . .
It might have been funny to them now that the presence
of Mrs. Rance and the Lutches—and with symptoms too
at that time less developed—had once, for their anxiety
and their prudence constituted a crisis; it might have been
funny that these ladies could ever have figured to their
imagination as a symbol of dangers vivid enough to precipitate the need of a remedy" (II, 253-54). It is by deliberate
references to its "first beginning" in the earlier conversation
that Maggie leads her father to the "present situation."
Her declaration: "When . . . you love in the most abysmal
and unutterable way of all—why then you 're beyond everything, and nothing can pull you down" (II, 262), tells
him much; but she tells him more by responding to his

disclaimer of jealousy with "a look that seemed to tell of things she could n't speak" (II, 264). Throughout the rest of the scene, it is by what she refrains from saying that Maggie does what she must do. As she rocks with dizziness under her father's observation after she has proclaimed herself as selfishly sacrificing him, she reflects that they are saving the situation "or at least she was: that was still the workable issue, she could say, as she felt her dizziness drop. She held herself hard; the thing was to be done, once for all, by her acting now where she stood" (II, 268). And so she manages, as she has managed all along, not to say what will be destructive, but to lead her father to the unspoken pact and the solemn embrace which end the scene. Much earlier, in the conversation between the Assinghams which ends Part I, Fanny has spoken of Maggie's having to gloss things over for her father and her dread of his possible discovery that she is doing so.

. . . She paused, staring at the vision.

It imparted itself even to Bob. "*Then* the fun would begin?" (I, 397).

The fun in Bob Assingham's crude sense is just what the Ververs refuse to begin; but it is hard to believe that at the end of the scene with Maggie Mr. Verver does not know of Maggie's deception as the basis of their pledges of mutual belief. At any rate, from this moment, he begins to co-operate with her to save "their present situation."

The word "funny" has been associated with the situation while it is still being presented from Amerigo's point of view in Part I. The Prince, in the conversation with Fanny Assingham, shortly after Charlotte's marriage, talks of Charlotte's being with him in Mr. Verver's boat. "She knew of course what he meant—how it had taken his father-in-law's great fortune, and taken no small slice, to surround him with an element in which, all too fatally weighted as he had originally been, he could pecuniarily float" (I, 268). The Prince feels that he and Charlotte have a common benefactor to bring them together, as if

Mr. Verver is her father-in-law too because he has saved them both. Then he challenges Fanny: "Don't you remember . . . how, the day she suddenly turned up for you, just before my wedding, we so frankly and funnily talked, in her presence, of the advisability for her of some good marriage? . . . Well, we really began then, as it seems to me, the work of placing her where she is" (I, 269).

After Charlotte's saying upon her return from her wedding trip to America that they have to do nothing at all, the Prince thinks: "Nothing stranger surely had ever happened to a conscientious, a well-meaning, a perfectly passive pair: no more extraordinary decree had ever been launched against such victims than this of forcing them against their will into a relation of mutual close contact that they had done everything to avoid" (I, 289). His actual use of the word "funny" comes a little later when he is reflecting that Mr. Verver takes "care of his relation to Maggie as he took care, and apparently always would, of everything else. He relieved him of all anxiety about his married life in the same manner in which he relieved him on the score of his bank-account. . . . It was a 'funny' situation—that is it was funny just as it stood. Their married life was in question, but the solution was n't less strikingly before them. It was all right for himself because Mr. Verver worked it so for Maggie's comfort, and it was all right for Maggie because he worked it so for her husband's" (I, 292-93). It is shortly after this reflection while he is pacing to and fro in boredom on a dreary afternoon that Charlotte comes to him with her question: "What else, my dear, what in the world else can we do?" (I, 297).

The Prince remains detached and reflective enough to use the word "funny" in considering Maggie's sense of responsibility about her father's party in Eaton Square. "The party was her father's party and its greater or smaller success was a question having for her all the importance of *his* importance; so that sympathy created for her a visible suspense, under pressure of which she bristled with

filial reference, with little filial recalls of expression, movement, tone. It was all unmistakeable, and as pretty as possible, if one would, and even as funny; but it put the pair so together, as undivided by the marriage of each that the Princess—*il n'y avait pas à dire*—might sit where she liked: she would still always in that house be irremediably Maggie Verver" (I, 323). The sting to his pride is clear; and yet he can find Maggie's apparently superior filial devotion pretty as well as funny.

He is thinking of an uglier sense of the word when he considers the world's judgment of the way the Ververs send him and Charlotte out alone together to represent the two households in society and finally send them off to the house party at Matcham. "They were exposed as much as one would to its being pronounced funny that they should, at such a rate, go about together—though on the other hand this consideration drew relief from the fact that, in their high conditions and with the easy tradition, the almost inspiring allowances, of the house in question, no individual line, however freely marked, was pronounced anything more than funny" (I, 330). His awareness of the possible "more than funny," the culpable, in his relation with Charlotte is the strongest impression of his use of the word; but there is no indication that he himself has yet begun to mount the tortuous staircase of his conscience to find the situation more—or less—than funny. After the houseparty he accepts the day at Gloucester with Charlotte as a "huge precious pearl" (I, 358) which has dropped into his hand as a reward for his boring himself so patiently and not snatching.

The transition from the Prince's rather cynically amused uses of the word to Maggie's tortured sense of the funny is made by Fanny in her report to Colonel Assingham of what has happened after the Matcham house party. When she says that Maggie has gone home instead of waiting for the Prince in Eaton Square, where she and her child "spread so," Bob's comment is:

"It *is* rather rum."

"That 's all I claim"—she seemed thankful for the word. "I don't say it 's any thing more—but it *is* distinctly, 'rum'."

Which after an instant the Colonel took up. " 'More'? What more *could* it be?"

"It could be that she 's unhappy and that she takes her funny little way of consoling herself" (I, 374).

The densest cluster of uses of the word "funny" occurs near the beginning of Part II when the novel has moved from the Prince's consciousness to Maggie's and she is trying to find some way of dealing with her suffering and bewilderment. As she receives Amerigo, on his return from Matcham and Gloucester, she refrains from letting . . . the truth on the subject of her behaviour . . . ring out. . . .

" 'Why, why' have I made this evening such a point of our not all dining together? Well, because I 've all day been so wanting you alone that I finally could n't bear it, and that there did n't seem any great reason why I should try to. *That* came to me—funny as it may at first sound, with all the things we 've so wonderfully got into the way of bearing for each other. You 've seemed these last days— I don't know what: more absent than ever before, too absent for us merely to go on so" (II, 18).

The apology in the "funny as it may sound" shows the extent of her feeling of deprivation. But the fact that she does not utter any such plea makes possible the tenderness of his embrace and the "tact" with which he treats the day at Gloucester. When he goes out to dress, she reflects on her own subjection to his personal power, and then her mind goes back to the conversation with her father at Fawns which had led to Charlotte's visit and all the consequences of that visit. Charlotte seems to her to have been brought in to help pull the family coach while she and her father are "seated inside together, dandling the Principino. . . . She had seen herself at last,

in the picture she was studying, suddenly jump from the coach" (II, 23-24).

At dinner she plies Amerigo with questions about Matcham and Gloucester at such a rate that he stares at her "visibly beguiled but at the same time not invisibly puzzled." His stare seems to suggest his saying to her that she need not pretend so hard; but she looks at him to show she is not pretending with "her lucid little plan in her eyes. She wanted him to understand from that very moment that she was going to be *with* him again, quite with *them,* together, as she doubtless had n't been since the 'funny' changes—that was really all one could call them— into which they had each, as for the sake of the others, too easily and too obligingly slipped" (II, 27). Maggie's choice of the word that deprecates the changes and yet tries not to take them too seriously is an example of the delicacy with which she picks her way as she starts to redeem the situation. But of course neither she nor her husband speaks any words aloud. Maggie simply yields to the unutterable sweetness of his embrace, which she *later* realizes "operated with him *instead* of the words he had n't uttered" (II, 28). One way in which James increases the sense of crisis in the whole evening is by presenting much of its progress through Maggie's later scrutiny of its details so that he seems to give at the same time the effect of the incidents as they first impress Maggie and as they come back to her heightened consciousness.

As she ponders "all the next day and all the next," the question comes to her: "What if I 've abandoned *them* . . .? What if I 've accepted too passively the funny form of our life?" (II, 25). Maggie's finding the same term the Prince has used to describe the whole situation brings into play again all of his attitudes which complicate the "funny form" for Maggie and with which she will now have to deal to create the true form of her marriage.

But before she can reach the true marriage of the final scene with Amerigo, she must experience all the pain

which is revealed as much in the vocabulary of the succeed-
ing books as in the violent images. She feels haunted,
"imprisoned" (II, 106), and thinks of Charlotte as
"doomed" (II, 283). Fanny sees her "strange grimace" (II,
114) and hears her tone that "might by this time have
shown a strangeness to match her smile" (II, 115) as she
speaks of her "danger." She feels herself "grimace" in
"weakness and pain" (II, 242) as she has the sensation of
being thrown over on her back with her neck broken by
the encounter with Charlotte on the terrace. She is conscious of Amerigo's "grimace" (II, 201) as he tells her she
is "deep" after her account of the bowl; and she thinks of
"his pale hard grimace" (II, 295) at the sound of Charlotte's
voice, which she herself hears as a wail, as the "shriek of
a soul in pain" (II, 292). The word "grimace," which
ordinarily suggests no more than wry amusement, is linked
wherever it occurs in the novel with pain or danger. The
words "pain" and "danger" constantly recur, as do "strange"
and "sinister." The strange becomes for Maggie even
"monstrous" and "lurid"; (II, 233) and the words "horror,"
"terror," "disgust" hover over the image of her finding
"evil seated all at its ease where she had only dreamed of
good" (II, 237). It is no longer possible for Maggie herself to call the situation "funny" in its oddity: "The dis-
guised solemnity, the prolonged futility of her search might
have been grotesque to a more ironic eye; but Maggie's
provision of irony, which we have taken for naturally
small, had never been so scant as now, and there were
moments when she watched with [Charlotte], thus unseen,
when the mere effect of being near her was to feel her own
heart in her throat, was to be almost moved to saying to
her: 'Hold on tight, my poor dear—without *too much*
terror—and it will all come out somehow'" (II, 284). She
does in truth have "different sorts of terrors" (II, 139).
One is simply that the couples will not be able to sustain
the pretense they are all making. "They learned fairly to
live in the perfunctory; they remained in it as many

hours of the day as might be; it took on finally the likeness of some spacious central chamber in a haunted house, a great overarched and overglazed rotunda where gaiety might reign, but the doors of which opened into sinister circular passages" (II, 288). With her father the pretense has to be of more than the perfunctory. In the strained conversation in which he seems to be testing her by speaking of their all being so happy, and especially his having "made Charlotte so happy" (II, 92), he forces poor Maggie to agree that "we certainly get nothing but the fun" (II, 91). But as he pursues his idea of their life, he makes the fun sound almost as sinister as it actually is for Maggie: "What it comes to, I dare say, is that there 's something haunting—as if it were a bit uncanny—in such a consciousness of our general comfort and privilege. . . . as if we were sitting about on divans, with pigtails, smoking opium and seeing visions" (II, 92).

The course of the "fun" in *The Golden Bowl* recalls Pinter's remark that "the point about tragedy is that it is *no longer funny.*"[7] The novel is perhaps not a tragedy; but the tragic force of the suffering is inescapable. Francis Fergusson has reminded us that the novel "feels tragic throughout" and that even in the final moment when Maggie "as for pity and dread" (II, 369) buries her eyes in Amerigo's breast, "authentic tragic emotion . . . is here, in the instant of vision and fulfillment itself."[8] One way in which James has intensified the feeling of tragedy is to show through the vocabulary the tragic evil and terror growing out of the funny.

7. Quoted by Martin Esslin, *The Theatre of the Absurd* (New York, 1961), p. 205.
8. *"The Golden Bowl* Revisited," *Sewanee Review,* LXIII (Winter, 1955), 26-27.

VIII ~ Conclusion

Henry James characteristically saw life as tragic. His letters, both published and unpublished, abound in expressions of its grimness as a fact to be acknowledged and somehow dealt with. In a letter of sympathy to Edith Wharton he writes, "but life is terrible, tragic, perverse and abysmal" (*Letters*, II, 91). The adjectives which surround "tragic" help to define it. The tragic emotion of terror and the sense of a fate which deals perversely with man lead to the climactic "abysmal." The feeling of the abyss most of all relates the suffering James is talking about to that of tragic drama, which is not only extreme in itself, but arises from situations which push man to the limits of his manhood—what Richard Sewall calls "boundary-situations."[1] In life, as in art, the people who most interest James are those who are capable of such suffering, those, "habitually ridden by the twin demons of imagination and observation,"[2] who because of their lucidity are responsible

1. *The Vision of Tragedy* (New Haven, 1959), p. 5. In a note Sewall gives credit to Ralph Harper for relating the phrase, borrowed from Karl Jaspers and other philosophers, to tragedy.
2. "The Special Type," *The Better Sort* (New York, 1903), p. 102.

moral agents and capable of decisions which are as irrevocably tragic as the surrounding circumstances are ironic.

In James's letters, the awareness of tragedy is relieved by the rich play of wit and comic invention. Often the gaiety seems dictated by a sheer sense of fun; but often (as in letters written during illness) it is quite openly used as a way to bear suffering. In an unpublished letter to Grace Norton, dated April 26, 1883, James writes with unusual candor about his deliberate assumption of cheerfulness: "You really take too melancholy a view of human life, & I cant afford—literally haven't the moral means—to hold intercourse with you on that basis. I am never in high spirits myself, & I can only get on by pretending that I am. But alas you *wont* pretend—that you are; & scarcely even that I am."[3] James is, of course, usually much more earnestly sympathetic with Grace Norton about the "terrible algebra" (*Letters*, I, 101) of her life; and in this letter of protest against her melancholy, he apologizes for his "beastly tone" and ends with the promise to come to see her and "make it all right" as soon as he returns from New York: "We will weep together or laugh together, or do neither; and I am always your intensely sympathetic

H. James"[4]

But in spite of the sympathy, or indeed exactly because of it, James's own need of the resources of comedy as defense is uppermost in this letter. Yet in the letter of July, 1883, in which he uses the phrase "terrible algebra" to describe Miss Norton's life, he can affirm that "life is the most valuable thing we know anything about, and it is therefore presumptively a great mistake to surrender it while there is any yet left in the cup" (*Letters*, I, 100). In the letter to Henry Adams written in March, 1914, less than two years before his own death, James confesses to a much more

3. James Papers, Houghton Library, Harvard University, b MS Am 1094, No. 939.
4. *Ibid.*

complicated use of comic pretense, one which itself reaches an affirmation of the value of life:

> I have your melancholy outpouring of the 7th, and I know not how better to acknowledge it than by the full recognition of its unmitigated blackness. *Of course* we are lone survivors, of course the past that was our lives is at the bottom of an abyss—if the abyss *has* any bottom; of course, too, there's no use talking unless one particularly *wants* to. But the purpose, almost, of my printed divagations [*Notes of a Son and Brother*] was to show you that one *can*, strange to say, still want to—or at least can behave as if one did. Behold me therefore so behaving—and apparently capable of continuing to do so. I still find my consciousness interesting—under *cultivation* of the interest. Cultivate it *with* me, dear Henry—that's what I hoped to make you do—to cultivate yours for all that it has in common with mine. *Why* mine yields an interest I don't know that I can tell you, but I don't challenge or quarrel with it—I encourage it with a ghastly grin. You see I still, in presence of life (or of what you deny to be such,) have re-actions—as many as possible—and the book I sent you is a proof of them. It's, I suppose, because I am that queer monster, the artist, an obstinate finality, an inexhaustible sensibility. Hence the reactions—appearances, memories, many things, go on playing upon it with consequences that I note and "enjoy" (grim word!) noting. It all takes doing—and I *do*. I believe I shall do yet again—it is still an act of life (*Letters*, II, 360-61).

There is a profound difference between the old pretending to be in high spirits as the only way to get on and the interest which James now encourages "with a ghastly grin," the reactions he has to " 'enjoy' (grim word!) noting." It is the doing, the pretending, the grim enjoying, which have become the act of life; and James no longer needs to make a separate assertion that "life is the most valuable thing we know anything about." Wanting to talk and behaving as if one wants to seem almost equated in the sentence in which these phrases occur. And the

interest is surely in part the cultivation itself in the sentence: "I still find my consciousness interesting—under *cultivation* of the interest." The "so behaving" has become the reality.

A letter to Edith Wharton in 1908 has an even more direct bearing on the uses of comedy in the tragic world of James's fiction: "Only sit tight yourself *and go through the movements of life.* That keeps up our connection with life—I mean of the immediate and apparent life; behind which, all the while, the deeper and darker and unapparent, in which things *really* happen to us, learns, under that hygiene, to stay in its place. Let it get out of its place and it swamps the scene; besides which its place, God knows, is enough for it! Live it all through, every inch of it—out of it something valuable will come—but live it ever so quietly; and—*je maintiens mon dire*—waitingly!" (*Letters,* II, 104-5).

Here again there is the pretending which becomes the reality; but the "it" in "Live it all through" seems to have become not "the immediate and apparent life," but "the deeper and darker and unapparent." James appears to be asserting that the "something valuable" will come both from going through the movements of outward life and from experiencing "the deeper and darker and unapparent" behind it. But the value of the darkness is unattainable if it is allowed to "swamp the scene." If this is reading too much into the passage, at least it is clear that James is talking about both the distinctness and the intimate interconnection of the immediate and apparent life and what lies behind it.

These passages throw light on the relation of comedy and tragedy in James's fiction. His fictional world was consistently tragic; but the place of comedy in such a world grew steadily more complicated and even ambiguous. After the time of his apprenticeship, he was regularly able to fit comedy naturally into surrounding tragedy; but in the early work it remained separable, an element used for

the specific purposes of contrast, satiric definition of the sources of evil, or affectionate mockery which gives reality to idealistic or romantic characters. These uses James was never to forego (just as he can still tell Edith Wharton to *"go through the movements of life"*); but in the late novels the comedy has become also an inseparable part of the tragic experience of the characters who even on the edge of the abyss find their "consciousness interesting."

The primary demand of comic response is the ability to take things in more than one way at a time. Almost from the beginning James makes this demand on his readers in conjunction with the demand of tragic involvement. It is also true that most of his centers of consciousness are from the beginning "affected with a certain high lucidity" (*The Art of the Novel*, p. 130). But his early idealists who suffer are themselves, for all their intelligence, devoid of a sense of comedy. The most extreme example perhaps is Olive Chancellor; but even Isabel Archer, who is capable of much more perceptive self-scrutiny and certainly finds her own "consciousness interesting" achieves no comic detachment from herself. In the early novels James often requires the comic point of view from the reader, but rarely from the principal character. (A notable exception to this generalization is Eugenia in *The Europeans,* who—as Richard Poirier has brilliantly demonstrated[5]—also gives tragic overtones to this novel which is otherwise one of the most wholly comic of James's fictions.) In the novels before the final period, it is less central figures to whom James gives a comic awareness as part of their tragic vision. Supporting characters like Ralph Touchett and Mitchy suggest the doubleness of attitude which will disturb the principal characters in the novels of the "major phase." The power of these characters to stand outside themselves and see both themselves and the besetting perversity of fate as ridiculous

5. *The Comic Sense of Henry James,* pp. 95-144, 230.

complicates and deepens their own suffering at the same time that it heightens the sense of tragedy for the reader. That Ralph is compelled to see himself as the instrument of the tragic irony of making Isabel an heiress and thus a desirable *parti* for Osmond is the final confirmation of his whole ironic view of life. " 'I believe I ruined you,' he wailed" (*The Portrait of a Lady,* II, 414). What makes the comedy tragic is his power to feel all the anguish of Isabel's punishment for her mistaken attempt to fulfill the "requirements" (I, 261, 265) of her imagination and thus of his own. He can *see* the irony as comic; but he *feels* it as tragic. Yet his last words are an assertion of faith: "I don't believe that such a generous mistake as yours can hurt you for more than a little." Then after her crying that she is happy, " 'And remember this,' he continued, 'that if you 've been hated you 've also been loved. Ah but, Isabel—*adored!'* " (II, 417). It is perhaps a measure of how much nearer James has come to the attitude of the last novels by the time of *The Awkward Age* that he allows Mitchy no such hope. Nanda's mistake too is generous; but Mitchy sees it as irrevocable. Instead of hoping that she will cease to be punished, he must rest in the assurance which he gives Mr. Longdon that her unsatisfied passion is itself "a life" (*The Awkward Age,* p. 482). For his own part instead of being allowed, like Ralph, to die, he must cope with little Aggie, who is now in "what 's universally recognised as [Mrs. Brookenham's] regular line" (p. 522) of giving advice to wives involved in adulterous liaisons. Nanda promises never to abandon him; but he must manage his own tragic comedy, and so he listens to her analysis of Aggie with an interest "even now not wholly unqualified with amusement" (p. 529). The problem of Aggie remains a partly comic complication. As he has said of Nanda's unsatisfied passion for Van, it is his passion for Nanda—unsatisfied even by a kiss of her hand—which must make his life. From such a double consciousness as Mitchy's, it is not a long step to the

complexities of tragic suffering and comic judgment in Strether, in Milly and Densher, and in Amerigo and Maggie. The complex consciousness of the protagonists is one of the principal causes of the famous ambiguity of the late novels. James regularly refers to comedy and tragedy together; and in the "project" for *The Ambassadors* which he submitted to Harpers', he shows them as indistinguishable when he speaks of: "The whole comedy, or tragedy, the drama, whatever we call it, of Strether's and Chad's encounter" (*Notebooks*, p. 401). James gives the late protagonists a kind of awareness of irony (a term which he often links with tragedy and comedy) which creates for them a special relation to the drama of such encounters. They are both tragically involved and comically detached enough to see the incongruity as comic. Since the ironies grow out of the characters' relation to manners the phrase "Tragedy of Manners" used by Constance Rourke and Frederick Crews[6] seems an apt description. The inner world "in which things *really* happen to us," is indeed dark and deep; but the surface which is consistently preserved is that of the comedy of manners. In *The Ambassadors* it is most of all in her struggle to preserve the comedy of appearances that the reality of Madame de Vionnet's tragedy is revealed to Strether. And Strether's enlightenment about himself, which is at once comic and tragic, is brought about by his having to reckon with new codes of manners and new relations between behavior and the reality behind it.

How tragic the comedy is in *The Wings of the Dove* is epitomized in Densher's finding something both "funny"[7] and fearful in his and Kate's "being so damned civil" to

6. Constance Rourke, *American Humor, A Study of the National Character* (New York, 1931), p. 256; Frederick C. Crews, *The Tragedy of Manners: Moral Drama in the Later Novels of Henry James* (New Haven, 1957).

7. *The Wings of the Dove*, Century Library Edition, p. 407. The substitution of the word "droll" in the New York Edition (II, 393-94), makes the incongruity even more striking.

each other. Even his deception of Milly, Kate has made
him see as an act of high civility, indeed of mercy. Kate's
"We 've gone too far. . . . Do you want to kill her?" (II,
199) shows all the truth of Milly's passion as well as the
monstrousness of their deceit. Yet at Milly's grand recep-
tion, where Kate wins Densher's consent to his rôle by
promising to come to his rooms, they can still speak of
what they are perpetrating in the manner of polite irony:
"Only, you see, one has to try a little hard to propose to a
dying girl" (II, 229). Though with part of his consciousness Densher feels the enormity of what they are plotting,
he is also still thinking partly of "those numerous ways of
being a fool that seemed so to abound for him" (II, 180)
and of making sure that for once he will be "master in
the conflict" (II, 231). The sense of being an "ass" (II,
209) which has dominated his comic judgment of himself
is turned to tragic enlightenment only by the final interview with the dying girl, which has made him feel "forgiven, dedicated, blessed" (II, 343). It is this same last
visit to Milly which transforms the dreadful comedy of his
pretense of love for her into the tragic reality so that Kate
finally tells him, "Her memory 's your love. You *want* no
other" (II, 405).

The Golden Bowl provides the supreme example
in James's fiction of going "through the movements . . .
of the immediate and apparent life" as a way of making
"the deeper and darker and unapparent in which things
really happen to us . . . stay in its place." The discrepancy
between the surface and the dark deeps underneath is here
most extreme, and so is the effort to act as if the discrepancy did not exist. The movements of life come to have
for Maggie the feeling of contortions, as the extravagance
of the imagery frequently emphasizes. And yet James
fulfills for her the promise he makes to Edith Wharton
that "out of it something valuable will come." Maggie
does manage to live her anguish "ever so quietly" even
when she feels most like a trapeze artist in the performance

of her surface comedy. She manages to resist saying the sentences which would shatter the scene of social and familial peace which she watches over the top of her unread French periodical as the others play cards in the lighted smoking room at Fawns. She is as much in a "boundary situation" as any tragic heroine; but she prefers the perilous comedy of good manners to the explosion of tragic crisis. The "something valuable" which comes to her out of this living quietly through all the deep, dark, unapparent suffering and going simultaneously through the movements of immediate and apparent life is the integrity of her own marriage and possibly that of Charlotte's marriage to her father.

The letter to Henry Adams shows how much of James's own sensibility he has given to these late protagonists. His own "ghastly grin" appears on their faces as a "grimace." He allows them to find their "consciousness interesting" and to "cultivate" the interest, though it involves acknowledging that "Everything 's terrible . . . in the heart of man" (*The Golden Bowl*, II, 349). Beyond the awareness of tragic comedy and the cultivation of interest which he allows his characters, what he suggests as the source of his own response to life is his being "that queer monster, the artist, an obstinate finality, an inexhaustible sensibility" so that he enjoys noting his reactions, in spite of the parenthesis " (grim word!)" with its comic— or tragic—self-mockery. The noting is the whole course of his fiction, the *doing* which is his "act of life."

Index

W9-CZT-683